D0771803

ADDICTION

~ A MOTHER'S STORY ~

My Son's Descent into Addiction

and Where It Took Us

<table>
<tr><td>

WARNING

Readers may find some of the language offensive. Unfortunately, addiction is not a "polite" disease and conversations with an addict often become disrespectful and offensive when the addict feels cornered in some way. The conversations have been presented in the manner in which they unfolded.

</td></tr>
</table>

JUNE ARIANO-JAKES

WARNING

Readers may find some of the language offensive. Unfortunately, addiction is not a "polite" disease and conversations with an addict often become disrespectful and offensive when the addict feels cornered in some way. The conversations have been presented in the manner in which they unfolded.

Copyright © 2012 June Ariano-Jakes

All rights reserved. No part of this book may be reproduced or transmitted in any form or by any means, electronic or mechanical, including photocopying and recording, or by any information storage or retrieval system without written permission from the author, except for brief passages quoted in a review.

Library and Archives Canada Cataloguing in Publication
Ariano-Jakes, June
Addiction : a mother's story : my son's descent into addiction and where it took us / June Ariano-Jakes.

ISBN 978-0-9867013-0-6

1. Ariano-Jakes, June. 2. Parents of drug addicts—British Columbia—Biography. 3. Drug Addicts—Family relationships—British Columbia. 4. Heroin abuse—British Columbia—Case studies. 5. Cocaine abuse—British Columbia—Case studies. I. Title.
HV5805.A75A3 2012   362.29'13092   C2001-906549-5

Editing by Dania Sheldon
Book design by Fiona Raven

First Printing, January 2012
Printed in United States of America

Published by Jaanue Publishing
www.AddictionAMothersStory.com

~ *Dedication* ~

You, my son, have taught me about the human spirit, the will to survive, and the unbelievable strengths we are capable of. Not a day goes by that you are not on my mind and in my heart.

To all of my children—thank you for allowing me those times, those years, of sharing your lives with me. Nothing takes away memories. They last forever. And as always, you are all on my mind and in my heart.

To Kare and Michael, who without question lead lives of absolute integrity. You have blessed my life over and over, and I have tremendous gratitude for your love, your respect, and all you have taught me.

To Jeff and Diane, our dear friends, who bless my life and are there, no matter what, and who love my children unconditionally. We are truly a family by choice.

To my parents, Pop and Gram, who are no longer with us, but who taught me by example that when the going gets tough, quitting is never an option. Not a day goes by that you are not in my thoughts.

To my brother and M.E., you bless my life with your love, kindness, support, and friendship.

To all people who struggle with addiction, may you find your way to the life you deserve, clean and sober, and with the knowledge, desire, and commitment to live the life you were meant to live.

To all the parents, brothers, sisters, husbands, wives, and children who walk the journey with an addicted loved one, may you one day see the view from the top of the mountain, with your loved one standing next to you, clean and sober, living the life you always wanted for them. May your lives finally be filled with the peace and serenity you so rightly deserve.

To those of you who have tragically lost your loved ones to addiction, I am truly, truly sorry for your loss. May you find a place of peace, knowing you did the very best you could with what you knew at that time. And may you feel acceptance that you really had no control over your loved one's addiction. You did not cause the addiction and you could not cure it. But you did the best that you could.

To my grandchildren and all children everywhere, may you one day live in a world where the disease of addiction is a distant memory, relegated to the pages of history books with other diseases whose treatments and cures have been found.

To Debbie Berezan Holmes of Surrey, B.C., who has worked with and dedicated so much of her life to helping at-risk teens, and to Maggi Henderson. Thank you both for taking the time to read my manuscript and give me your thoughts based on your experience, knowledge, and awareness of addiction. I am so grateful to have you both in my life.

To my editor, Dania Sheldon, of Gabriola Island, B.C. Thank you so much for your dedication to excellence, your advice, and your encouragement every step of the way. You have become a true blessing in my life.

To Fiona Raven of Vancouver, B.C. for your artistic excellence in design and for all your advice and suggestions. Thank you very much for your dedication to working until everything felt right, with such patience and consideration. You have touched my heart.

To Claire Sowerbutt of C.S. Communications Ltd. in Vancouver, B.C. for helping me, a complete computer illiterate, design and set up my blog and Facebook sites, and showing me how to use them, with so much patience and humour. Thank you so much.

And finally, I want to acknowledge two truly good people who walked into my life over thirty years ago and from whom, because of my own fears and insecurities, I walked away. I have truly learned over the years that certain people who are absolute treasures will enter our lives. They teach us something real, and we should hang on to those treasures because they really do leave their footprints on our hearts. And those footprints last forever. So to J. Pat Reid and to Elaine Pace, thank you for influencing my life and teaching me a huge lesson I needed to learn. Wherever you are, "I hope your trail in life has been good to you."

CONTENTS

I MET THE DEVIL—
HIS NAME WAS ADDICTION

"Life is not the way it's supposed to be. It's the way it is.
The way you deal with it is what makes the difference."

~ VIRGINIA SATIR ~

ADDICTION IS A DISEASE, A VERY COMPLICATED DISEASE. IT eventually becomes a severe health problem as well as a serious criminal justice problem. You cannot be a drug addict and not also be a criminal.

The cost of addiction is staggering.

Addicts are not "bad" people. They are "sick" people who do "bad" things. There is a difference. We remember the good person underneath the addiction and we desperately want him or her back.

My son is a heroin and cocaine injecting drug addict. He is polite, charming, and handsome. He is kind and he is generous. He also lies, steals, manipulates, and uses good people. He has robbed banks. He has been in and out of detox facilities probably four dozen times over the years. He has been in more than two dozen recovery houses and programs. He has also been in treatment centers in both Canada and the USA. He has been in prison.

Only my son has the power to change his circumstances. Ultimately, it is his choice.

He is currently in another treatment facility. I no longer have expectations that a miracle will happen, but I always have *hope*. Hope that this will be the time he finds those missing pieces he needs to feel whole.

He is my son and I love him deeply.

This is the story of my journey as the mom of a hard-core drug addict, navigating the road of his addiction.

If you have picked up my book, then we are probably soul sisters or you are a soul brother with children battling the same disease.

We may have come from different backgrounds, but our journey, yours and mine, will be the same. We will walk similar paths for many years. Why? Because we love our children and we will never give up on them.

We will cry the same tears. We will say the same prayers. We will make the same deals with God.

As parents, we often blame ourselves, in spite of knowing we did the best we could. Why? Because we think, "If I did such a good job, how could this have happened? I had to have done something wrong."

You didn't!

You did not cause this disease and you can't cure it. The addict is the only person with the power to do that. All that we have control over is how we will allow this horrific situation to impact us. *Tough stuff.* We cannot change the addict in our life. We have to change how we have been allowing their behavior to impact us.

Easy?

Not at all. Nothing will be harder. The addict is the only one who "is in control of being out of control," if that makes sense. Sometimes it takes years to get to the point of realizing *we have no control—that we finally regain control.* We at last start to take back our power.

Remember, you are being held *hostage to addiction.* It really is up to you to decide when you will not pay any more ransom.

We have given all we can, physically, emotionally, spiritually, and financially. This journey has become more difficult and heartbreaking than we could have possibly imagined. We have no control at all as to how the journey may end. It is like being a passenger in a car without a steering wheel. The choice you have to make is whether or not to remain in that car.

The path our addicted loved ones are on is completely destructive to them, to you, to your entire family, and to anyone else they can take along for the ride.

Because there are no quick fixes, day after day we try to figure out how to break through that shell of addiction that is keeping them trapped. All we want is for them to be okay. In the eyes of the law they are criminals. To us they are a part of who we are. They are our children.

We are powerless over their addiction but we are not powerless in absolute terms. If we are to survive this disease called addiction and to help those we love, we have to hang on to or regain our power.

We know we are losing battles left, right, and center, trying to help our addicted loved ones find their way, but we must not forget ourselves in that mix.

We have lost the people we were. We have lost years of peace, wanting our children to be okay when clearly they weren't. We have lost our innocence as to what we believed human beings were capable of.

We always knew there were the good, the bad, and the ugly. We just never really imagined that the bad could possibly be so ugly, that the drug dealers, smugglers, traffickers, and kingpins in the drug trade would have no conscience and would do anything and everything conceivable to make money, in turn destroying the very people we love so much.

As parents we often walk around softly, trying so hard not to "set them off." When we find ourselves changing our behaviors in such ways, we have given our addicted loved one our power or sense of control. Power in the wrong hands is dangerous and, in all too many cases, deadly.

Only you can make the decisions about what you feel comfortable doing or not doing. There are no easy answers. What works for one may not work for another. However, if whatever you have been doing has not brought you the results you need, then it's time to try another strategy. Remember, if we keep doing the same thing, how can we expect different results?

It's time to get out of our comfort zone. I know how difficult this is. It took me more years than I care to remember before I began to make changes. For every two steps forward, I took one step back. Sometimes for every one step forward, I took two or three steps back.

This journey we are on is devastating. It is gut-wrenching. The road is full of potholes and washouts, and each day brings new challenges and new heartbreaks. Each day also brings *hope and awareness*, and a reminder that the human spirit has the strength to change and the ability to do so.

~

I remember waiting at the terminal building as my son walked off the ferry from Vancouver Island. It was Christmas Eve. Nathan was thirty-five years old, and two and a half hours earlier he had been released from Williamhead Penitentiary, a federal correctional institution outside of Victoria, British Columbia, Canada. He had been incarcerated for a series of bank robberies. It was not his first incarceration, nor his first time at Williamhead. Each time, though, I prayed it would be the last.

Over the course of nineteen years, my son has seen the inside of many Canadian municipal, provincial, and federal correctional institutions, as well as one in Texas.

My son is a drug addict. Today he is clean and sober, but a drug addict can never, ever let his guard down because he will always be a drug addict. Addiction is a disease you never escape. That is a fact. Nathan has to live with that fact and so do I.

As parents, we rock and calm them when they cry as infants. We kiss their hurts when they fall down as toddlers, and those kisses make it better. We do everything we can to help our children. We work extra hours so that they can have the same outfits as the other kids at school, and when they're teenagers we sit up with them after a date to talk about what a great time they had. Weeks later, we sit while our child cries in our arms because that same person who rocked their world now wants to break up. So we hold them while they cry until the sun comes up, and eventually they fall asleep on our lap. We gently move their head to their pillows, cover them with their favorite blanket, and tiptoe out the door. We are parents, and as parents we know how to fix things for our children. After all, we have been doing it since the day they were born.

Enter drugs.

Drugs infected the lives of your child, my child, the kids next door, or maybe three doors over. For some it was recreational use. Exploration. A party. They could use or stop when they wanted to. They could go on to other things, visiting the drug scene occasionally or not again. But not our kids. Something was different. Why were they not stopping?

This was the start of *their* lifelong journey. This was the start of *our* lifelong journey.

Why?

Because there was a difference between our children and the kids next door. For those others, drugs became a form of recreation. But to our children, addiction had raised its ugly head. Together, we and our children were in for a voyage that would take us to places we could not have imagined, even in our worst nightmares.

For the first time as a parent, this was something I could not fix or kiss and make better.

I had met the devil and his name was Addiction.

THE BIGGEST MISTAKE OF MY LIFE

*"If you have made mistakes, even serious ones, there is always
another chance for you. What we call failure is not
the falling down but the staying down."*

~ MARY PICKFORD ~

"Life is a succession of lessons which must be lived to be understood."

~ HELEN KELLER ~

*N*ATHAN AND FOUR OF HIS FRIENDS WERE HUDDLED IN THE BATHROOM
in deep discussion. The door was open so I walked in. They all looked
very worried, and I knew something was wrong. I remember saying, "Guys,
whatever is bothering you, maybe I can help, but please don't tell me it's drugs."

Their faces dropped. That was the moment nineteen years ago when my
life changed forever. I didn't realize it at the time because I was still in that
mode of "I am Nathan's mom—we'll be able to fix this."

Nathan and his friends had met a guy at a McDonald's. It could have
been anywhere, it just happened to be there. He asked them whether they
wanted to make some quick money. All they had to do was deliver a parcel to
a bar on the Canadian side of the US/Canada border by Blaine, Washington

and collect some money that would be waiting. They delivered the parcel, but the guy at the bar told them to come back later and he would have the money. Of course, he never did come back, and Nathan and the other guys were supposed to meet up with some "Spanish-speaking guys" at 7:00 p.m. with the cash. They had no way of getting the money to cover it, and they were terrified and panicking in my bathroom.

At that moment I made the biggest mistake of my life, one I have regretted every single day for nineteen years. It was to be the first of many mistakes I made in the name of love.

I should have gone immediately to the police, but that did not enter my mind at the time. It really didn't. All I could think of was trying to help Nathan get the money to pay off these obvious gangsters so they wouldn't come after my son.

I cashed in my paychecks, borrowed against my credit card, and got the money they needed and the promise from Nathan that this would never, ever happen again. The fear, then relief in their eyes convinced me this would be the first and very last time.

What an idiot I was. All that did was get them a pat on the back for a job well done, and an implicit promise of bigger money if they would do it just one more time. It made Nathan feel important. Here was an older guy telling him he had done a good job and patting him on the back. This stroked his ego, and the promise of lots of money clouded every moral he had ever been taught and shown.

The next time they were paid in cash and cocaine, and Nathan's life changed forever. So did his friend Alex's. They became hostages to addiction. The three others were heavy users, but for them it was a party and they could walk away. Eventually they did, and years later one became a plumber, one a doctor, and the third a policeman.

Where did addiction take my beautiful son? Where did his addiction take me? Where did addiction take our family, who love Nathan so much?

Addiction eventually took him to the bowels of hell, and we were along for the ride.

As I look back on what I have learned from many mistakes over many years, I realize we truly are the authors of our own lives. Each and every day, we start a new chapter. We can't change our past, can't change the decisions or the choices of yesterday. We have to acknowledge them, accept them as decisions we made with the information we had at that time.

Don't beat yourself up. Whatever you did yesterday to handle your loved one's addiction, whether you gave him or her money, paid the rent, made excuses, *let it go*. That was yesterday. Today you can make different choices. Today you can hold that person accountable. You are accountable only for the choices you make. *You* are the author of your own story.

When we allow ourselves to be manipulated out of feelings of guilt or pity, thinking this is what love is about, we allow someone else to be in control of that chapter in our story.

Hold on to your power.

WHO WAS TO KNOW THAT SUCH A GENTLE SOUL WOULD ONE DAY LIVE IN SUCH A VIOLENT WORLD?

"Be kind, for everyone you meet is fighting a great battle."

~ PHILO OF ALEXANDRIA ~

*N*ATHAN IS THE SECOND OLDEST OF MY FIVE CHILDREN, AND over the years his life has tumbled into complete and utter despair. The journey was a long, hard one.

First, though, let me give you a little background information. Perhaps your child is very much like mine.

Nathan was always a kind and gentle soul. As a child, he brought home lost kittens and dogs, hid turtles under his bed on a stormy night so "the thunder wouldn't scare them outside." He once caught a fish in the lake near our home but could not kill it. He brought the fish home, filled the bathtub with water, and set the fish free in it. He put in some food and thought the fish could live there forever. Well, it did until I almost had a heart attack when I went into the bathroom in the middle of the night!!

Nathan brought home a kitten he had found all alone in the snow, and a dog with three legs. He said the dog smelled bad so it probably didn't have anyone to look after it. Since it was the middle of winter, I agreed the dog could stay in the porch, just for the night. It really did smell awful. Of course, in the morning the three-legged dog was asleep on his bed. We never did find its owner, and it seemed to have decided ours was an acceptable home and stayed all winter. But that was Nathan.

Who was to know that such a gentle soul would one day live in such a violent world?

I never, ever saw that coming.

~ 4 ~

FAMILY BACKGROUND

"You gain strength, courage and confidence by every experience
in which you really stop and look fear in the face. . . .
You must do the thing you think you cannot do."

~ ELEANOR ROOSEVELT ~

Nathan's dad and I were married for seven years. I was seventeen when we married and Dan was twenty-six. The marriage ended not from anyone's fault. There was no good guy or bad guy. We simply matured in completely different directions.

We had three beautiful children together: Kiara, Nathan, and Jada. The children lived primarily with me but had dinner every Wednesday night with their dad and spent every second weekend with him.

Dan's was the "fun house"—movies, company, sleepovers, weekends watching their dad play hockey, and going out of town. His was definitely a more affluent lifestyle. Nathan and his sisters always had a fun time, but what Nathan craved more than anything was time with his dad just doing father-son "buddy" things. They didn't have that one-on-one kind of relationship, but they always did fun things with a larger group of people. His dad always loved him, but for some reason Nathan never felt loved enough.

Everyone's needs are different and as parents we honestly try to fill those individual needs, but sometimes we aren't even aware they exist.

~

Our home was much more basic. Homework, studying, Brownies, judo, baseball games, early to bed because they had school the following day.

We often had pancakes for supper, poured in different shapes. One night we had pancakes shape like ducks. Another night it might be turtles or elephants. We were really struggling financially, although the kids have since told me they never realized it. *But* they don't eat pancakes anymore!!

One Easter weekend a number of coworkers got together for a barbeque. I had never particularly noticed Bernie until he mentioned to me that the Kool-Aid jug was empty and the kids would probably want more. That was what captured my heart—this man concerned about my children having more Kool-Aid. I was smitten. Oh, the reasons we women fall for guys!!

The positive male presence that I thought I had found over the Kool-Aid jug was a sham. He proved to be a cruel, abusive person. I was making plans to leave with my children when I found I was pregnant with Jasmine. Like so many women before me and so many women after me, I stayed because I was sure being a father would change him. He would see what real love was and understand why children and their parents have this deep connection. But of course, that never happened, and I became pregnant once again.

Our two children, Jasmine (Jazz) and Michael, were as beautiful as Kiara, Nathan, and Jada. They were born fifteen months apart and, like their sisters and brother, they were the center of my universe.

My beautiful son Michael was born when I was just five and a half months pregnant. He was eleven inches long and weighed only one pound, twelve ounces. He spent four and a half months in a neonatal intensive care unit until he was finally able to come home. At that point he weighed less than Nathan had at birth.

Nathan was thrilled to have a little brother.

~

I remember once hearing that you can always tell a man's character by how he treats his mother and how he treats his dog. I wish I had heard that earlier. Bernie called his parents "peasants," and he abused small animals, kicking our brand new puppy down the stairs and out into a blizzard because it had peed on the floor. Kiara, Nathan, Jada, and I got our coats and boots on and ran outside to find the puppy. The snow was blowing so hard we could not even see any tracks. We searched and searched well into the night in the blowing snow but never did find our little puppy. We knew it must have crawled away and died or got buried under the snow.

Eventually Bernie got another dog. Again, it was a small dog that he could easily control. He often submerged that little dog in a rain barrel as a form of discipline. We were constantly running out, begging him to please leave Jessie alone. Jazz in particular loved little Jessie and this abuse devastated her.

Bernie's job took him out of town approximately fifteen days a month and every one of us counted down to those days he would be away. My children and I were not allowed to have friends over when he was home, and his verbal abuse was constant and unrelenting.

I prayed the profound love I had for my children would compensate for Bernie's negative behavior. But of course, it doesn't work that way.

I sat in the bleachers at every baseball, judo, and soccer practice and game, and every swimming lesson my children went to. We ate our meals together and they did their homework every night at the kitchen table. They entered projects in the annual science fair and took music lessons. I never missed a single parent-teacher interview, school pageant, concert, or music recital. Being a mother meant everything in the world to me.

My children never left the house without a hug and an "I love you," and they never went to bed without me tucking them in with an "I love you— happy dreams." Nothing meant more to me than being a mom.

Deciding to stay in the marriage for as long as I did, trying to make it work, was a huge mistake and my children and I suffered immensely because of that decision. It was my responsibility to ensure that no one in my children's lives would treat them with such disdain and so critically, and I own that blame. That is one thing I will never ever forgive myself for until the day I die. Bernie did a lot of damage to each and every one of us in different ways before I finally told him he had to leave for good. There would be no more chances. I no longer believed his promises that he would change.

~

I feel it is important to note that family dynamics, or situations of emotional or mental neglect or abuse, do not in themselves cause addiction. At the same time, studies have repeatedly shown that the majority of addicts have suffered sexual, physical, or emotional abuse as children. It is also important to note that relationships within a family unit often determine feelings of self-worth and self-love, or lack of the same.

~

When Nathan was thirteen years old, we moved to another city. On Kiara's sixteenth birthday and just a month before Nathan was to turn fourteen, he was hit by a truck when he ran to cross the street after getting off a bus.

It was 9:10 p.m., he was ten minutes late getting home, and I walked down the block to look for him. I saw an ambulance and police car arriving up ahead. I ran faster than I had ever run in my life. Somehow I knew it was my son.

The impact threw him eighty feet, onto the other side of the highway. Nathan came out of surgery at 5:30 the following morning. His left kidney, spleen, and left lung had all been damaged. His heart was bruised. His ribs were all broken, as were his left knee cap and tibia. He had nerve damage to his entire left side and lacerations over a good portion of his body. A couple of days later, he developed sepsis and became extremely ill. His temperature was dangerously high, and he went into congestive heart failure.

Kiara, although just sixteen, looked after her sisters Jada and Jazz, and baby brother Michael, all the while studying for exams, while I stayed around the clock at the hospital with Nathan.

During this time, Nathan was given morphine, then Demerol, and later Tylenol 3 with codeine, for pain. Years later, he told me he liked the feeling he got during that time from the pain medication. The susceptibility for addiction was already swirling around in him. But I didn't know.

Nathan spent several weeks in the hospital and the next year in physiotherapy five days a week. He still finished that school year with seven and a half out of eight school credits. I was really proud of him.

Nathan was now fifteen and asked to go and live with Dan for the next school year. He said he really wanted to try and develop a closer relationship with his dad.

I knew this was what Nathan really wanted—what he needed or thought he needed. Unfortunately, that year did not go well. Nathan ended up getting only half of one school credit, failing the seven and a half other classes. He was also drinking a lot. Dan kicked Nathan out and I begged him to come home, but he adamantly refused, saying it was just a matter of time before he would be back in his dad's home.

Unfortunately, Nathan was befriended by a group of taxi drivers who hung out in front of the bars late at night, waiting to pick up fares. They introduced him to different substances and his addiction took off. By the time I convinced Nathan to come home, the grounding, if you will, of his addiction was set. He went from one abusive substance to another.

His step-father, not surprisingly, did nothing to help or encourage Nathan. Quite the opposite. He did everything to push Nathan's buttons and it was a constant battle.

One afternoon, when Michael was four years old, he had a cold and a sore throat. He coughed and the lozenge he was sucking on fell out. Bernie grabbed Michael and yelled at him about wasting money. Nathan snatched

Michael away from him and said, "If you ever touch my brother again, I will fucking kill you." Bernie knew Nathan meant it. Bernie only picked on the weak link. For the first time, Nathan had stepped up to Bernie and Bernie was scared.

One night as I was lying awake, waiting for Nathan to come home, I was asking God, as I did every night, to please keep an angel on his shoulder, when Bernie said, "I hope the police find him dead in a ditch."

Oh, how I hated that man. I hated him and I feared him, but when I look back now, as a strong, independent woman, in control of her destiny, I wonder how I could ever have allowed someone such as that near me—and more importantly, anywhere near my children. I take full responsibility for the harm caused, because I allowed someone like that to slither so insidiously into our world that before I knew it, our lives were not our own anymore.

5

DRUG TRAFFICKERS ARE LIKE PEDOPHILES

"You must take personal responsibility. You cannot change the circumstances, the seasons, or the wind, but you can change yourself. That is something you have charge of."

~ JIM ROHN ~

*A*S PARENTS, WE TRY TO RAISE ALL OUR CHILDREN THE SAME. We love and care about them, and try to meet their individual needs. Nathan was looking for that adult male figure he had pictured in his mind. He found it in the drug trade, or so he thought. But he was lost. He went searching but became a pawn in a terrible game that took him on a horrific journey of unbelievable pain, suffering, anxiety, and loss. Many, many losses.

~

A drug dealer, a drug trafficker, an importer, they are like pedophiles in that they seek out the weaker personality. Just as a pedophile looks for vulnerable children, so does the trafficker. They groom their victims, they boost their egos, they sit and talk to them—like Nathan and his buddies making the "friend" at McDonald's.

These people know how to play the game, and it is a very, very dangerous game that destroys lives, families, communities. These individuals know how to pump egos, build false confidence, and use our children to do their dirty work, in the process sucking our children in to where they think there is no way out. Millions worldwide never escape.

Every country has its gangs. Many cross borders, as do the major biker gangs—those who believe these are just a bunch of good old boys who every December ride their Harleys in the Christmas Motorcycle Toy Run, bringing stuffed teddy bears to the less fortunate, need to give their heads a shake. Did you ever stop to think that many of those less fortunate children receiving those teddy bears are less fortunate because their parents are struggling with drug addiction from the drugs supplied by the very people who may have donated that teddy bear? That's the reality.

Now please don't get me wrong—many bikers and "weekend warriors" every year join that toy run with hearts in it for the right reasons. They are honest, hard-working, morally and socially conscious men and women who love their bikes and participate because they care about less privileged children, and this is a wonderful, fun event for them. I'm talking about the biker gang members who use this as a public relations stunt.

There are gangs and organizations around the world, in every country, involved in the drug trade—the Italian mafia, the Russian mafia, the Mexican and Columbian drug cartels, the Chinese triads, the Polish mob, the Jewish mafia, the Irish mob, the British crime firms, the Vietnamese gangs, the South Asian gangs, to name a few.

We have branches of these organization right on our own doorsteps, in Canada and in the USA. We have the Hell's Angels, Independent Soldiers, United Nations Gang, Indian Posse, Native Syndicate, Mad Kowz, Big Circle Boys, 14K Triad, Wah Ching, Bloods, Crips, Mara Salvatrucha (better known as MS-13), Rock Machine, Public Enemy No. 1 . . . and the list goes on and on. It seems endless.

To a parent of an addict, to law-abiding citizens, they are the lowest of the low. They are the bottom-feeders of society, because all they care about is the money. They live in big houses and drive fancy cars and throw money around like water, while the individuals who have made them rich live in absolute misery. The sicker they make you, the richer they become. They care about one thing: the bottom line.

~

I will say right up front though—the decision to use and continue to use drugs remains the sole responsibility of the drug addict, of our addicted loved ones. My son, your son or your daughter, they are responsible for their addiction. They initially made a moral choice and that was to use a potentially addictive substance for their own pleasure.

Of course, they never anticipated that they would become addicts, that once addiction took its hold they would feel "powerless" over it. However, they *are not* powerless. Sobriety is within their grasp. They can become clean and sober. It is a choice to use narcotics. But—and this is the fifty billion dollar question—if it is a choice (and no one would willingly choose to become an addict), what is it that makes addiction so powerful that so many simply seem incapable of making that transition from a using addict to an addict in recovery?

~

I remember the day Nathan came over freshly showered and shaved and dressed up. I asked him where he was going. His comment was, "You don't want to know." I knew he was in a bad situation, and he was there in the hope that I would pull the information out of him.

He had a drug debt he could not pay. A huge debt. He had been told to take the bus to point A, get on a second bus to point B, and there someone would pick him up and take him blindfolded to a warehouse, where he would do a porn movie.

This was devastating to him. Nathan is an addict but he is a gentle soul and respects women. However, he was told if he did not show up at point A by 1:00 p.m. he would be dead by 7:00 p.m. He saw no choice, believed there was no option. The debt was too huge.

I explained to him that he could not go there under any circumstances, that if he owed that much money and they were taking him blindfolded to a warehouse, this was no soft-porn video they were planning on making. This was a snuff video and someone was going to die. There was no way I was letting him go. I bought him a one-way bus ticket out of town and he stayed away for several months.

I don't know all the things my son had to do to pay for his addiction, I only know that anything of any value eventually disappeared—cash, credit cards, jewelry, musical instruments, snowboards, bikes, power tools; all could be used, sold, or traded for drugs.

I remember Nathan coming home without his new jeans. Without his driver's license. Without his social insurance card. A drug dealer will take anything you have that can be sold or traded or held as collateral.

Often dealers will allow our loved ones to run up debts they know cannot possibly be paid; then they have the victims in their pockets. When you can't pay, you end up stealing cars or breaking into jewelry stores or driving through the front window of a camera or computer store. That kind of thing. It's not the big guys doing this. These crimes are committed by addicts who have to pay off a debt—or else. They are our sons and daughters.

A hot commodity is a truck, not because they want the truck but because it can be used to smash through the front entrance into a place, load up with whatever that particular shop sells, and be gone. The stolen articles are taken to a warehouse, then the truck gets dumped. Stolen cars go to chop shops.

The guys getting caught smuggling drugs across the border are not the bigwigs. Those aren't the guys making a fortune off our addicted sons and daughters. Those *are* our addicted sons and daughters, who have huge debts to pay and therefore become the mules. The people taking the greatest risk of getting caught are our teen or adult children, yours and mine. To the traffickers, they are expendable. Their only value lies in what they take over and what they bring back.

Addicted people are genuinely suffering. As I have said, no one wants to be an addict. No one ever expected to find him- or herself in that position. But each made choices and the repercussions of those choices became addiction. Except for the very rare horror stories, no one ever forced our loved ones to use drugs. They made a personal choice to get high. That personal choice started them on this journey and we have no control over it. No power. No influence.

Yet we are along for this dark, dangerous, gut-wrenching, and heartbreaking ride to the bowels of hell. We are on a rollercoaster and there are no brakes. We cannot stop this chaos. Their actions, their choices, their behaviors—all are out of our control. But while we have no control over our addicted loved ones' addiction, we do have control over how we will play out our role in this deadly disease trajectory.

Wishing for something won't make it happen. When we are talking about addiction, all the wishing in the world won't make a bit of difference. It won't change our loved one's behavior and it won't change us. *Change takes work.*

There is a wonderful prayer said at all the meetings of Narcotics Anonymous, Alcoholics Anonymous, Nar-Anon, and Al-Anon. It is called the Serenity Prayer:

> *God, grant me the serenity*
> *to accept the things I cannot change,*
> *the courage to change the things I can,*
> *and the wisdom to know the difference.*

Know the difference!! Remember this prayer. Say it, believe it, live it.

My son's addiction took him from the mean streets of Vancouver, Canada to the mean streets of Baton Rouge, Louisiana and many places in between.

There is no misery, no pain and suffering, no human despair in North America like the mean streets of any city in these countries.

Everyone has their own story of how and why they got there, and why they are still there.

6

NATHAN LOVES HIS FAMILY,
BUT HE LOVES DRUGS MORE

"The me in the mirror is not what I once was. The me in the mirror
is not the final word on who I will become.
The me in the mirror is simply a reflection of today."

~ GLEN A. HASCALL ~

FROM THE TIME NATHAN WAS SIXTEEN AND DRUGS BECAME his focus, he tried many times to walk away from that lifestyle, always to be sucked back in.

Over the years, I have mortgaged and remortgaged my home, maxed out credit cards, used up an inheritance from my dad, and sold off possessions to the tune of $460,000. I was willing to do anything to keep my son alive and find him the help he so desperately needed.

Nathan has been in some of the best treatment centers here in Canada and some of the best recovery houses in the Vancouver area. He has been in detox in Canada several dozen times over the years and in a medical detox facility in Florida. He has also been in a treatment center in Louisiana. Everything and anything I could do to keep my son alive meant one more day that he might find his way.

Through all these years and all that treatment, his addiction was so powerful that he always went back to it. Its pull, his love affair with cocaine and heroin, was so powerful that when he was emotionally hurting, nothing and no one came before it.

Nathan has always loved his family and has been deeply loved by Kiara, Jada, Jazz, Michael, and me. His love for us is real and deep. But it has never been as real or deep as his love of the drugs. That is the way of the addicts in our lives. The pull of the drugs outweighs the pull of the family. That is our reality, yours and mine.

You and I and all those others who walk our path will understand that *Happy* Mother's Day or *Happy* Birthday or *Merry* Christmas don't sound like appropriate wishes, because even though we "put on the happy" for others to see, inside we are carrying so much pain and heartache.

A happy birthday for most people is reflected in the gifts and party, and how many people call to send wishes. But for us, *happy* is if our children remember to call or show up, if we are not at the hospital because of a suicide attempt or an overdose, or if the police are not knocking on our door. A *happy* day for us is just knowing where our children are. That may mean that your child is asleep on the couch for the night. At least you know where he is and what he's doing, and so, for that night, you have a better sleep. It may be only one night, but that's better than the alternative. Instead of sending happy birthday wishes, we say, "I hope your day was *peaceful*." For us, a peaceful day means more than all the treasures of the world, all the happy birthday calls, and all the store-bought gifts.

And so, my friend, I hope and pray that this year will bring you more peaceful days. You certainly deserve it.

~ 7 ~

UNLESS YOU WALK A MILE
IN SOMEONE'S SHOES . . .

"There isn't a cloud so thick
that the sun isn't shining on the other side."

~ AUTHOR UNKNOWN ~

MANY YEARS AGO, I WALKED INTO MY FIRST NAR-ANON MEET-ing. For those of you who may not be familiar with Nar-Anon, it is similar to the more widely known Al-Anon, but Nar-Anon meetings are for the families of loved ones struggling with the disease of drug addiction.

The first time I walked through those doors, there was a group of women laughing. It made me think that they could not have as worrisome a problem as I did because I could see nothing about addiction to laugh at.

Boy, was I wrong. Once our discussion started, I quickly realized that for the women in that group, like myself, the worries and behaviors related to our loved one's addiction were driving us all to our knees.

I soon learned that, indeed, if we didn't laugh, we would cry. So sometimes we laughed and sometimes we cried. Actually, a lot of times we cried. I cried for the load they were carrying and they cried for the load I was carrying. We were a sisterhood. We understood like no one else could, because unless you walk a mile in someone else's shoes, you can never fully comprehend their journey.

Some meetings we were able to vent. Some meetings we were able to accept addiction as a disease, and sometimes we felt free to curse that disease.

However we felt, it was okay by everyone else in the room. We were safe. There was a genuine caring, love, compassion, and understanding in those meetings. We never knew each other's last names because of the right to anonymity, but when we entered that room, we knew were with the best friends we would ever have.

Below is a list of questions to ask yourself if you suspect drug use or if you wonder whether you would benefit by attending a Nar-Anon meeting. Try and answer as honestly as you can. If you find you are answering yes to even a few of these questions, Nar-Anon might be able to help give you the answers you are looking for.

~ Do you find yourself making excuses or trying to cover up for your loved one's behavior?

~ Do you find yourself questioning their honesty in response to your questions?

~ Is your child missing classes or is there a clear change in their school performance?

~ Is money disappearing?

~ Does there seem to be a number of new friends that you haven't been introduced to or that your teen has not brought by?

~ Is your loved one more argumentative, beyond what might be perceived as teenage behavior?

~ Is your loved one irritated much more easily and by seemingly minute matters?

~ Are they not where they say they are going to be?

~ Are you catching them in lies?

~ Do you find you are "walking on eggshells" so as not to upset them or have them fly into a rage?

~ Do you find yourself feeling concerned or worried about their behavior—perhaps causing you to feel anxious or upset?

You have absolutely nothing to lose and everything to gain by reaching out for help and information.

If you have never been to a Nar-Anon meeting, I urge you to look up a meeting in your area and walk through the most welcoming door you will ever find. If you cannot find a Nar-Anon meeting, call or e-mail:

World Service Organization
Nar-Anon Family Group Headquarters, Inc.
22527 Crenshaw Blvd. Suite 200B
Torrance, CA 90505-3071 USA

Phone: 1-800-477-6291 or 310-534-8188

Or

E-mail: wso@nar-anon.org

Or you can call any Narcotics Anonymous and they will direct you to the correct place.

Attending that first meeting was the best thing I did for myself. Nar-Anon meetings allowed me to find a bit of solace and sanity in the insane world of addiction.

BOY, DID I GET A DOSE OF HUMILITY

"Never look down on anybody unless you're helping them up."

~ THE REVEREND JESSE JACKSON ~

REMEMBER AT ONE NAR-ANON MEETING MANY YEARS AGO, one mother spoke about her son's addiction to heroin and what it had done to the family. Her greatest heartbreak was that she now had a second child battling addiction. It floored her because she could not understand why, after seeing what addiction had already done to his brother and the family, this second child would have even considered using, only to go down the same path.

I'll be honest. At that time I remember thinking, "I wonder what this mother is doing wrong."

Boy, did I get a dose of humility.

It wasn't long before *I* had a second loved one into the cocaine scene: my beautiful niece Sara, who was now living with us. It completely blindsided me. Nathan, Sara, and Jada were inseparable growing up and they shared many friends in common. Jada and Sara had always been genuinely concerned about Nathan's continuing drug use, and as a family we were united in the common goal of Nathan achieving sobriety.

Now, those of us who walk this journey all know that addicts or drug users are liars. Sorry, but it is a fact. If your child is using drugs or your child is an addict, accept the fact that he or she is also a liar. Addicts need to be. They always have to cover their tracks. It turned out that Sara's concern about Nathan was actually a smokescreen to hide her own drug use.

It became an uphill battle to get my niece away from that scene and the addict she eloped with while embedded in that lifestyle. It took two years of devastation and heartbreak, restraining orders, and police and fire department involvement. Her husband slashed the bedroom mattress, as well as all her shoes and clothing, and carved up her furniture with a knife.

I was relentless. I went to the police each and every time another incident occurred where I felt his behavior threatened my niece's safety. She hated me for it, but I was not going to lose this beautiful girl, whom I loved so much, to drugs or violence.

Fortunately, after two years she tired of that lifestyle and was able to completely walk away and not look back. She divorced and eventually remarried.

The difference between Nathan and Sara is that for Sara, it was more the excitement of the "party," whereas Nathan was already long addicted. Unlike his three buddies huddled in the bathroom with him that long-ago day, he wasn't able to just walk away.

GRAM HAD LOU GEHRIG'S DISEASE
AND NATHAN WAS UNABLE TO BE
PHYSICALLY OR EMOTIONALLY PRESENT

"The three Rs: respect for self, respect for others,
and taking responsibility for all your actions."

~ AUTHOR UNKNOWN ~

THE LAST FEW MONTHS OF MY MOTHER'S LIFE, SHE LIVED HERE
with us. Gram was always a highly independent and proud lady
who worked very hard all her life. Sadly, at sixty-nine years old she passed
from ALS (amyotrophic lateral sclerosis), more commonly known as Lou
Gehrig's disease. ALS is a devastating neurological disease that eventually left her unable to walk, talk, move, or swallow. Throughout all of that,
Gram's sharp mind, quick wit, and sense of humor remained.

Gram wanted to die at home with us instead of in hospital. On Christmas Eve, 1996, she went into a coma at 4:00 in the afternoon. My brother
Keith, who had been trying all day to get a flight, finally arrived from back
east. She loved all five of her children but she had a special place in her heart
for Keith, and it came as no surprise that when he arrived from the airport

and walked to her bedside, she knew he was there and opened her eyes to see him one last time before slipping back into a coma.

Nathan was in a treatment center at that time. We were in the middle of the snow storm of all snow storms, and here two RCMP officers were at my door. The officers asked whether Nathan was here. They said a month earlier, Nathan and a friend of his had passed counterfeit $100 bills at a gas station. All I could do was apologize to them for my son and give them the date he would be getting out of the treatment center and coming home. I then returned to my mom's room to care for her.

We had converted our living room into a bright bedroom for Gram so she could be downstairs. My brother Graham and I stayed with her around the clock for the last several days. One of us was always awake and by her bedside. We made a good team caring for her. Mom stayed in the coma throughout Christmas Day, and she died with us all beside her at 11:50 a.m. on Boxing Day. She opened her eyes very briefly as if to get permission to leave us. We told her to go towards the light. She had that look that said, "Thanks for looking after me—I'm ready to go now."

Over the years, so many life-altering circumstances entered our lives, but Nathan was unable to be physically or emotionally present. That is what drug addiction does. An addict simply becomes indifferent to anyone else's suffering.

Ten months later, when we spread Gram's ashes, Nathan was in an Ontario jail for stealing a car.

~

Over the years, as Nathan got deeper and deeper into the lifestyle of his addiction, life became one crisis after another, one tragedy after another, and each time I lost more of myself as I tried to find a way to help my son. I just could not seem to grasp the concept that I was powerless over his addiction. My thinking was, "I'm his mother, for God's sake—it's my role as a mom to help my child. What am I missing? Certainly if I am a good mother, I should be able to save my son from this." I kept trying to rescue him. But how do you save someone from himself? That is part of the insanity of drug addiction.

I made many, many mistakes in the name of love. To me, loving meant helping, nurturing, caring, understanding, being there when he needed me, being supportive and trusting, assisting and lending, giving and forgiving.

Do you see the insanity of my thinking? I believed that whatever it took to "help" him would make him see how much he was loved and cared about. That is how distorted your reasoning can become when someone's addiction consumes your every waking hour. You don't say, "I am powerless over this." Instead, you think you just haven't found the solution yet. And what happens? You become so obsessed with helping them that they don't need to help themselves. *You* take care of the problems.

When they don't have enough money for rent, or food, or bus fare, or whatever, you become the go-to person and you somehow feel that you are helping. I know, because I did that . . . over and over and over again. And it was the *wrong* thing to do. It was wrong on every level.

Addiction, although it is a disease, cannot be "treated" like other diseases.

My mom did absolutely nothing to develop ALS. Children's hospitals all over the world are filled with sweet, innocent little children with horrible, life-threatening conditions. They have done absolutely nothing wrong and yet they suffer. Their parents suffer and would trade places with their children in a heartbeat if it meant eliminating one day of their suffering. Patients go through dialysis and wait for kidneys. Others are waiting for hearts or lungs or livers, suffering and dying, hoping for a donor. These are the sorts of diseases that require our loving, nurturing, assisting and caring, gentle, understanding selves. The people suffering horribly from these diseases would almost certainly do anything in their power to help themselves get well, whatever it took. And yet, all too often their illnesses are completely out of their control.

Addiction is a disease but it falls into a completely different category and as a result, we as the parents of addicts have to deal with this disease differently.

In the case of addiction, all too often, helping hurts. With addiction, when we think we are being kind, we are actually being cruel, because we help to keep our addicted loved ones where they are. And they definitely love us for it!!!

If by being kind we are actually being cruel, then the flip side is that often when we feel we are being mean by not "helping" addicts—when we hold them accountable for their actions and they hate us for that—we are actually taking the kindest action we can.

~

The relationship between a drug addict and his or her drug(s) of choice is comparable to that of a marionette and its puppet master. The puppet master pulls the strings to get the marionette to do whatever he wants; drugs completely control the addict's life.

So often, we too find ourselves in the position of marionette, with our addicted loved one as the "puppet master." The addict has in essence taken control of our lives, our happiness, and our sense of peace.

When the addict we love continues using, we become so obsessed with "helping him get better" that the goal becomes all consuming. The reality is, we have absolutely no control in the situation, no power to prevent it from recurring over and over, and no power to stop his destructive behavior. We *cannot* fix this problem. We must accept it is completely out of our control.

The only power we have is to determine whether we will let their addiction control us. We can't change the addict but we can change how we will—or won't—allow ourselves to be controlled by the addiction. Just as the addict has learned what works and what doesn't in terms of manipulating us, so have we learned. So now it is time to say, "I cannot change you. I have tried everything I can possibly think of, but I have no power over you and your addiction. None. *But* [and this is where we begin to change], I do have power over my thinking, over my actions, and over what I will allow."

Did I start doing this early on? No, I didn't. I stayed in the rescue mode far too long and I will always regret that. My heart was in the right place. I only wanted to help. But remember what I said: where addiction is concerned, helping all too often hurts because it just prolongs the inevitable. Drug use doesn't slow down for addicts. They require ever more to achieve a high. They develop a tolerance that fuels the need for more drugs, more often. When the frequency and the amount increase, so do the inevitable debt and the resulting violence.

~ 10 ~

JUST ONE OF MANY BEATINGS

*"Because your own strength is unequal to the task, do not assume that
it is beyond the powers of man; but if anything is within the powers and
province of man, believe that it is within your own compass also."*

~ MARCUS AURELIUS ANTONINUS ~

THERE WERE TIMES OVER THE YEARS THAT ADDICTION TOOK an especially terrible toll on Nathan. In the world of drug use, unpaid debt has serious repercussions.

I remember Nathan coming home beaten so badly he was unrecognizable. His face was black and blue, swollen beyond belief, his nose was broken, his jaw dislocated, his teeth all loose. His eyes were bleeding and he could not hear out of one ear. His body was battered and bruised from being repeatedly kicked.

He refused to call the police and lay a charge against his aggressor. I could not do that for him, as anything I said would be considered hearsay.

All that for an $80 drug debt he owed a "friend." Only $80!!

We teach our children that no one has the right to hurt them, and yet the greatest harm to addicts is by their own hands, their own choices.

LITTLE BROTHERS ONLY SEE
WHAT THEY KNOW

"Whoever you are, there is some younger person who thinks
you are perfect. That there is some work that will never be done
if you don't do it. There is someone who would miss you
if you were gone. There is a place that you alone can fill."

~ JACOB M. BRAUDE ~

NATHAN LOVED HIS LITTLE BROTHER MICHAEL FROM THE moment he was born, and Michael adored his big brother. Whenever Nathan lay down on the couch, Michael would climb up and lie there with him. The two brothers were inseparable when Nathan was home.

By the time Michael was in kindergarten, Nathan was using heavily. A lot of the time, cocaine psychosis was evident. Nathan had not come home for a few days and I was very worried. On this particular day, when I was going to drive down to the school to pick up Jazz and Michael, like I did every day at that time, Nathan came out of the hedge at the side of the house. I told Nathan to go inside, that I would be back in a few minutes. He insisted he needed to come. He had no shirt on and was somewhat disheveled, but he promised if I let him come he would stay in the van. I did not want Jazz and Michael to be upset or embarrassed.

I went to the classroom to pick up Michael, when Nathan suddenly appeared by my side. The other parents backed away slightly, but little brothers only see what they know, and Michael was thrilled that his big brother had come to get him from school. He jumped into Nathan's arms and away they went to the van while I waited for Jazz. At that time, it seemed Nathan was not a danger to anyone but himself.

That is part of the denial of addiction for both the addict and those who love him. We still see that gentle child holding the puppy. In reality, a drug addict *is* always a danger to everyone around him, in one way or another.

Back home on the couch, Nathan stretched out and, as addicts often do, was sweating from the effects of the drug. But Michael never saw the addict, he just saw his big brother who adored him. Michael didn't have that kind of relationship with his father. He got more love and attention from a drugged out brother in one day than he got from his father in a lifetime.

~

Once again, we hadn't seen Nathan in a couple of days when Michael said his eyes were itchy, not in the eyes themselves but rather on the eyelids. They were clearly red and irritated, so I took Michael up to the walk-in clinic.

The doctor said he had microscopic lice at the base of his eyelashes. I had never heard of this in my life and I was horrified. We would have to use a magnifying glass and pull out each louse with tiny tweezers, as nothing chemical could be used around Michael's eyes.

The next two hours were spent trying to extract the lice without hurting Michael and without pulling out his eyelashes. Because of all he had gone through as a premature infant, he had a higher pain tolerance level than most and he sat there like a trooper, unflinching, letting us do what had to be done.

After Michael was completely taken care of, I went to check everyone else's hair but no one had any sign of lice. He could have picked this up at school, I thought. A note had come home the previous week about lice being detected on two students in his classroom, advising parents to double check their children's hair, which I had. I wondered whether it could have come from Nathan, whether perhaps he had contracted lice from one of the places he frequented in his quest for drugs.

Around midnight, Nathan arrived home in a drug-related stupor. I sat him down and looked in his hair, and sure enough, it was crawling with lice. I thought I would vomit. I told Nathan he had to get into the bathroom immediately and wash his hair and body with lice killing shampoo, but he was so out of it he could not follow directions. It was all I could do to get him into the bathroom, as he kept nodding off. My only option was to put him in the bathtub myself and delouse him, tears streaming down my cheeks. All I could think of was, *What can I do to save my son from his own actions?*

~ 12 ~

I FELT I HAD JUST SHAKEN
THE HAND OF THE DEVIL HIMSELF

"It's not the load that breaks you down, it's the way you carry it."

~ LENA HORNE ~

NATHAN STARTED TALKING ABOUT A GUY NAMED "SNAKE," AN addict in recovery about twenty years older than himself—so about my age. Snake had taken Nathan under his wing, he said. I was very concerned about this relationship, with its obvious age gap.

I asked Nathan to bring Snake around so I could meet him. Nathan seemed in awe of this guy, gushing about him and all his accomplishments, how Snake was helping him, and that they wanted to get a place together that they would make drug-free. Nathan believed this would be a perfect relationship of two guys helping each other to stay clean.

In a perfect world, he might have been right.

The next day, Nathan brought Snake around to meet me. When I stretched out my hand to shake his, a chill ran right through my body. I felt I had just shaken the hand of the devil himself. Snake backed off the step, ready to leave with Nathan. I called Nathan back inside and begged him not to go.

You and I know that we women do have a sixth sense. Everything in me was saying to keep Nathan away from this man. But Nathan was adamant Snake was going to "save" him.

"No, Nathan, he will use you and hurt you. Please believe me."

"Mom, you're wrong about him. He's a really good person. I have to go, Mom."

"Please, Nathan, no."

Despite my begging, Nathan went with him and they found an apartment to rent. They made an agreement that if either started using, the other could move out without further responsibility. They each contributed $400 to the rent.

One night about a week later, Nathan called. "Mom, can you come and get me? This place is a fucking crack house. I've been cleaning up their mess and their puke for three straight days. I want to come home."

I told him I would be right there and help him get his belongings.

He said, "No, Mom, I don't want you in there. I'll meet you on the sidewalk."

Everything Snake had said, everything he had promised Nathan, was part of a "recruitment," I believe. He was not the "savior" he professed to be. He was pulling Nathan into his world of drugs and crime. He was an "associate" of a well-known biker gang with chapters around the world.

Nathan came home but, unbeknownst to me, he was receiving threats from Snake about owing for the next month's rent, even though they had made an agreement that if one used the other could leave. To make matters worse, while Nathan was living with Snake, he lost his job.

One night about two weeks later, I got a call from a "friend" of Nathan. He'd heard that Snake had stabbed Nathan and that was all he knew. I was panic-stricken. I called everyone I knew who knew Nathan. They all said the same thing, but no one could say where my son was.

I was devastated and went into rescue mode, searching every place and hideout where I thought Nathan might be. I searched along the railway tracks and under the train trestles. I searched behind buildings in areas I was scared to go. But my son was hurt and I had to find him.

I spent the entire night searching. Nothing.

I went home, hoping there was a message on the answering machine, but the only messages were from people calling about Nathan.

I was just heading out the door again when I heard Nathan's voice on the machine. I grabbed the phone. He said he couldn't come home because it would put all of us in danger. I urged him to tell me where he was. Eventually he did and I picked him up. He had been stabbed five times in the legs and his body was a wreck. I wanted to take him to the hospital and call the police, but he refused, saying that if the police got involved, Snake would kill him.

Snake wanted money from Nathan, but the amount wasn't $400 anymore—he told Nathan that if he did not come up with $700 by 5:00 p.m. that afternoon, "I know where your mother lives." Nathan was terrified. This was not about rent. This was extortion. Snake was not just after Nathan, now he would come after the family. Nathan was desperate and so was I. I had four other children, and two of my daughters worked night shifts. They could be easy targets of an evil man.

I made another mistake and listened to Nathan, who insisted he'd be a dead man if the police got involved. So I took him home and cleaned and dressed all his wounds, then I went to the bank to get $700. At 5:00 p.m., he met Snake at the designated spot, gave him the money, and walked away. He had seen true evil, seen Snake for what he was.

The last thing Nathan heard, Snake was wearing cement boots at the bottom of the Fraser River. He didn't know whether it was true or not, but either way it had no effect on him. Nothing anyone could do surprised Nathan anymore.

As his mom, I felt that nothing could shock or surprise me anymore either. I had shaken the hand of the devil and I had seen the gates of hell. Or so I thought.

13

COMMIT TO CHANGE—
IT'S TIME TO REGAIN OUR POWER

*"Right now you are one choice away from a new beginning—
one that leads you toward becoming the fullest human being you can be."*

~ OPRAH WINFREY ~

A HARDCORE ADDICT KNOWS WHAT IT MEANS TO LIVE IN absolute poverty. Homelessness, hunger, sickness, violence, and degradation are part of what addicts allow in order to accommodate their need or desire for their drug of choice. They live a very sad, lonely existence.

They give up everything for their addiction: family, friends, jobs, home, security, self-respect—their moral compass. This can all come back to them, but it takes work, commitment, and an absolute desire to change, to reclaim their lives.

I liken the battle an addict has with his addiction to that of a gladiator in the Colosseum: if you expect to get out alive, you have to fight like hell. Only one is going to win, the addict or the addiction. That is a brutal fact.

We cannot do it for them. All the love in the world will not make an addict stop using. The only person who has the power to change is the addict himself.

I heard a saying once that stuck in my memory bank. I don't know who said it but it went something like this: "You don't drown by falling in the water; you drown by staying there." If we continue in situations like drug addiction and refuse to do whatever it takes to get out of them, then we get the worst of what can happen. This goes for both the addict in our lives and those of us who love that person.

Just like our addicted loved one, we must make an absolute commitment to change. We need to let go of past habits. Whatever we have been doing to "save" our loved one isn't working. We have learned what doesn't work, so it's time to move on. We have to let go of the belief that we can change the addict's behavior.

We must make the same commitment we hope our addicted loved one will—the commitment to change what we have been doing. We start our own recovery to being the best we can be, in spite of the decisions of the addict whom we love so much.

Raise your standards. If you keep doing what you've always done, nothing will change. Instead, surround yourself with people who understand what you are going through. People who, like yourself, are trying to climb out of that dark place or who already have climbed out and are making positive changes. You will meet people who will inspire you, who are walking the same journey you are on, at Nar-Anon and Al-Anon meetings everywhere. One of the sayings at meetings is, "You have to go there to know there."

It is time to take care of yourself too. You have spent so much of yourself on your addicted loved one that you have lost yourself in all the chaos. Just for tonight, turn off the phone and get a sound sleep. Call up a friend you haven't seen for awhile and whom you miss. Go for a walk along the beach or river. Make a cup of tea and sit out in the sunshine. It is time to take care of you.

You will probably have to relearn this. When we become so all-consumed with helping our loved ones, we put ourselves at the bottom of the pile, feeling almost guilty at being happy when someone we love is in so much pain.

It is time to regain your power. Grab it. Hold it tightly. Never let it go. Taking care of you isn't selfish. It is imperative.

14

ANOTHER DANGEROUS
AND HORRIBLE "FRIENDSHIP"

"Character—the willingness to accept responsibility
for one's own life—is the source from which self-respect springs."

~ JOHN DIDION ~

ADDICTS HANG OUT WITH OTHER ADDICTS BECAUSE TOGETHER they justify each other's behavior. These are not friends. They are simply people who travel along together on the same road of destruction, heartache, broken promises, broken dreams, and broken people.

Real friends, on the other hand, bring out the best in us. They encourage, they build up, they never tear down. They help us on our journey to happiness and truth, and they encourage us to be the best we can be.

Nathan had a dangerous "friendship" with Steve.

Steve had good parents and a grandmother who loved him dearly. But nothing was ever enough for Steve. Food, clothing, cars, drugs, constantly getting in fights—everything had to be in excess, it seemed. Absolutely everything. And he was very smooth—too smooth and too charming.

Whenever Steve was around, Nathan was the worst for it. Steve always had a lot of money, which he would spend on a lot of cocaine, enough for him and Nathan to binge for days and days. Some of his behaviors scared Nathan; Steve's wasn't normal thinking, even for an addict. I noticed Nathan more and more distancing himself from Steve, and that was a relief for me.

Nathan hadn't seen Steve for a couple of months when he dropped by. He brought a really nice girl, introducing her as his girlfriend. She was ladylike, very different from the girls he had connected with before. I was concerned about her, hoping she was aware of who Steve could be. I felt that as a mom, I should give her a warning the next time I saw her, but I never did see her again. Nathan heard she had broken up with Steve.

No one broke up with Steve. He broke up with them.

One night, Nathan came home and said he had heard that Steve had taken this young lady up into the mountains to talk. But when they got up the mountain and away from everyone, he forced her to strip and dance around a campfire he had made, all the while shooting a gun at her feet. When he had one bullet left he shoved the gun in her mouth. Fortunately, it didn't fire.

Terrified, this girl was able to run into the forest and hide as he was trying to reload the gun. She hid in the darkness all night, alone and terrified he would find her. At daylight she was able to make her way to a logging road, where she was rescued.

Steve was eventually picked up, charged, and sentenced to prison. He had an attitude that would push a lot of buttons, and Nathan heard that "this big man on the outside wasn't so big on the inside."

I have often thought of that young girl. I can't imagine the nightmares she must have had and perhaps still endures. I hope she was able to eventually come to terms with this horrific event and to find happiness in her life.

We have since heard Steve died. He was a very dangerous person and he touched Nathan's life. But I feel bad for his parents. They had tried.

~ 15 ~

EACH TIME I THOUGHT HE'D REACHED
HIS BOTTOM, HE HADN'T

"I am not bound to win, but I am bound to be true.
I am not bound to succeed, but I am bound to live up to what light I have."

~ ABRAHAM LINCOLN ~

WHENEVER NATHAN APPEARED TO HIT HIS ROCK BOTTOM, I WAS
there to say, "Time to get you into a treatment centre or a recovery
house." Most times, he fought tooth and nail against going, but when I said
there was no more help unless he went, he would begrudgingly go.

Of course, it never worked because he hadn't reached that level to grasp
and be open to what was being said, what was being taught; or perhaps it
was just that he had not reached his bottom. I eventually came to realize
that his bottom was farther down than anything I could have imagined.
It really did reach the gates of hell. What he allowed himself to suffer was
beyond what I thought anyone would accept into their world. But he gave
the drugs permission.

Over the years, he was kicked out, or to put it more gently, "asked to
leave" every recovery house he entered. In the earlier years he would do

really well for a couple of weeks, then he would sabotage himself. Out he would go and back to using.

He went to what is probably the most respected and effective treatment centre in Canada, Edgewood, in Nanaimo on Vancouver Island. Again, I took out a loan against my home to cover the cost of the program.

As with any program or treatment centre I am aware of, you pay up front. If the client leaves against all advice, that is not the facility's fault—that is the client's decision and the risk taken by those who pay. After being there forty-nine days, Nathan was asked to leave for getting into a physical altercation. That was the longest he had ever stayed in a program and I was hopeful that he had absorbed something, even though he had not completed the program. I hoped the information was stored in his memory bank.

It was easy to stay clean in an environment where you were safe and semi-confined. There were no drugs, there were no drug dealers, there was no fear of violence, there was no crime. The staff gave all the help and guidance and encouragement possible in a safe, healthy, comfortable environment. He was out of harm's way—until he walked out the door and the real world hit him in the face.

Those who had really grabbed the tools given to them in the program stood a chance. Those who hadn't . . . good luck.

~

Nathan would generally be semi-willing to go into treatment when his safety was at risk, when someone from the "dark side" was after him, when threats were close to becoming his reality. I had to jump at those opportunities, hoping that maybe this would be the time Nathan found himself.

But that never seemed to happen.

The years passed and the date really didn't matter anymore. I couldn't even begin to keep track of the exact year when Nathan had gone into a program or walked out the door. There were just so many times. Each admission to a detox facility would be followed by entering a recovery house or treatment center. But it was never long before out the door he would go.

The only things that seemed to really matter to Nathan were how to get the money for the drugs, thinking about the drugs, shooting them, feeling them, and needing them again and again and again. Heroin and cocaine became his dearest love and there was nothing he wouldn't do for them.

~ 16 ~

SO MANY LOSSES, SO MANY DEATHS, AND A PSYCHOSIS THAT WOULD LAST DAYS

"It is not that some people have willpower and some don't.
It is that some people are ready to change and others are not."

~ JAMES GORDON, M.D. ~

NATHAN LOST A LOT OF FRIENDS TO OVERDOSE, SUICIDE, and accidents—or they simply disappeared. Had they been murdered? Had they met the same fate as Snake, at the bottom of a river?

Hopefully, some who vanished found their way to the other side and were able to fight and win that uphill battle out of addiction, moving on and never to be heard from again in that previous world. Hopefully.

~

A girlfriend of Nathan walked along the Trans Canada Highway in a stupor one dark, rainy night and stepped out in front of an 18-wheeler. There isn't much left of a person when she collides with an 18-wheeler. Nathan crumbled. His world fell apart. He was devastated.

~

A friend hung himself in his closet. Nathan never fully believed that this was a suicide—he wondered whether it was murder. It bothered him for years.

~

His best friend, Tyler, asked Nathan to drive into Vancouver with him to pick up some money. That day was to be a huge turning point in Nathan's drug use. Absolutely nothing could have prepared him for what was to happen.

Nathan waited in the car while Tyler went into the restaurant and picked up a shoebox containing $14,000. It was supposed to pay off some drug dealers, and Tyler was to take care of it.

He picked up the box of money and, as I understand it, on the drive back, both Tyler and Nathan shot up heroin. When they got to Tyler's house he didn't look well, and Nathan asked whether he could take him to the hospital. Tyler said no, that he would be okay. He was not able to walk on his own, so Nathan helped him into the house, got him settled on the couch, and brought the box of money in. He asked Tyler again whether he wanted to go to the hospital, but Tyler assured him he was going to be all right.

Should Nathan have realized how dire the situation was?

Perhaps.

But did he?

Absolutely not, and sometime after he left, Tyler died and Nathan never saw his best friend again.

Tyler's family and all their mutual friends blamed Nathan for Tyler's death. Even though they knew Nathan loved Tyler, they were grieving and angry, and believed he had left Tyler to die of an overdose.

Nathan received death threats. He could not go back to his apartment, could not walk down the street. He was devastated that his best friend was gone, yet he could not attend his funeral and he never got to say goodbye.

It took a couple of months for the autopsy results to all come back. The cause of death was a ruptured pancreas. All the years of heavy drug use had beaten up his body on the inside as well as the outside. Tyler's death changed Nathan's life forever.

~

"Mom, I'm at St. Paul's Hospital, they're locking me up, come and help me." That was the message on my answering machine.

I immediately got in my truck and began the one-hour trip into Vancouver. When I arrived, I checked in at Emergency. The attendant called over a security guard, who took me to a locked ward. He rang a buzzer and a nurse came to let me in.

I went toward my son. He was in a heavy, drug-induced psychosis. I had seen him in a psychosis before, when he was sure police and security guards were after him and was convinced every car on our street had officers watching him, ready to shoot. I had gone to the window and tried to explain to him that those cars belonged to the people in the houses along the street, but he had grabbed me and thrown me to the floor, covering my body with his.

"I won't let them get you, Mom, stay down!" he yelled, then got up and continued walking back and forth.

But the psychosis this time was deeper, much deeper than I had seen before, and it took several days for him to come out of it. We weren't sure he would.

Apparently he had gone to a coffee shop and, in his psychosis, believed that all of Tyler's family were there, even Tyler's elderly grandparents, and they were waiting to kill him, still holding him responsible for Tyler's death.

He also believed the doctor in this closed ward was not really a doctor but one of their friends, and he was going to inject him with something to kill him.

He was convinced the other patients in the emergency ward were people who had beaten each other up so they could get into the hospital and kill him. To Nathan, everyone around was a part of the plot.

The sprinkler system was really there to spray a gas at him. The smoke detectors were listening devices. His whole reality was obscured. He was agitated, up and down, standing on his bed in an attempt to deactivate the "listening devices."

"Don't leave me, Mom. As long as you're here they won't hurt me, but if you leave, you'll never see me alive again."

Eventually, he had to be restrained for his own safety. It took four security guards, two nurses, and myself.

He looked at me with tears streaming down his face.

"No, Mom, no."

I held him, knowing there was no choice, tears streaming down my face as well. I remember they were so salty they burned my cheeks and fell on Nathan as I held him.

Hours passed. The psychosis should have subsided by then, but one day turned into two, then two into three. He was now completely incoherent, child-like. Here was my beautiful son, in his mid-twenties, strapped to a bed, trying to speak, but making no sense and looking very confused.

What had been in the drug he had taken? Why was he not coming out of this?

Kiara, his oldest sister, sat at his bedside. She loved her brother but she hated his addiction and what it did to him and to the family. Kiara would tell Nathan honestly and right to his face what she thought of his addiction. He loved her and always respected her, probably because she never said anything behind his back that she wouldn't say directly to him. He was always a little intimidated by Kiara because he knew she called it like she saw it. There was no cushioning the reality.

Kiara held his hand and he chewed on her bracelet. Kiara never let people see her cry, but watching her brother brought her to her knees. She tried to brush the tears away so as not to upset me, but her heartbreak was raw and there was no denying it.

On the fourth day, Nathan started coming out of the psychosis. Kiara and I noticed a peacefulness beginning to settle over him; for the first time in several days, his face was not contorted in any way and his body was not spastic. He was quiet. Eventually, the restraints were removed and that pleased him—he smiled. It took several more hours before he became coherent.

He had no memory of the last four days. The last thing he remembered was going into the coffee shop after injecting just outside the shop door.

The doctor and an addictions counselor came in to see Nathan. They told him they didn't know whether he was going to come out of this. They said this was an absolute warning. Every time he used, he now risked going down that same path, until one day there would be no return.

I was convinced this had to be his bottom. He had to be ready for treatment. I spoke to the addiction counselor at length, and I asked Nathan whether, if I could make arrangements, he would go into treatment. He clearly was not keen on it but eventually agreed.

I called the credit card company from the ferry terminal, asking whether they could please increase my credit limit. I explained I had to get my son into treatment. The approval came through and we were on our way to the Orchard Treatment Center on Bowen Island, Canada.

The Orchard was a wonderful place, warm and inviting, and they tried everything to keep Nathan there, but four days later, after a box of new clothes I had sent for him arrived, he hopped on the ferry and came back to the mainland, back to the mean streets of Vancouver.

Again, I had given what I truly believed was a "hand up," when in reality it ended up being a "hand out."

WE CANNOT CONTROL THE ADDICT ANY MORE THAN WE CAN CONTROL THE WEATHER

*"You have to have confidence in your ability
and then be tough enough to follow through."*

~ ROSALYN CARTER ~

I WILL SAY THIS AGAIN FOR ONE REASON AND ONE REASON only—because I cannot stress it enough: it has taken me years to realize I am powerless over my son's addiction. Completely powerless. That is a horrible feeling to have.

To watch someone you love, so deeply, abusing his mind and body, becoming so completely ill, and to know he can get well if he would only stop his behavior, is devastating. To all of you parents going through the addiction of your child, regardless of his or her age, I feel and know your agony, the most horrible, helpless feeling in the world. It is like we are throwing a lifeline and all they have to do is grab it but they refuse.

Eventually, we come to realize this. It often takes a long time, years and years perhaps, as it did in my case. Only by finally recognizing and accepting that our "habit of helping" simply isn't working at all for anyone do we finally realize that change *on the addict's part* is the only option.

~

The addicts in our lives must take responsibility for their choices in order to move forward.

Equally important is that we must take responsibility for our actions and our own lives. You are the only person in charge of you.

All too often, our happiness, joy, health, and peace are dependent on the state of our loved one's addiction.

It is time to reclaim our lives.

Unfortunately, our loved ones may never get clean and sober. That is a sad reality and absolutely tragic because it doesn't have to be that way. But it may be our reality. They will ultimately decide their own fate in that regard.

What we must do next is imperative, because it is the only thing we do have the power to do. We have to reclaim our own lives.

Now we have to say this and mean it without exception: "I cannot allow your addiction to ruin my life any further. Your decision to use has kept me hostage. I am now taking my life back. I cannot control your life and I will not allow your behavior to control mine any longer. What we have been doing doesn't work. It's over. Today we start with new rules."

$$\sim\ 18\ \sim$$

ADDICTS ARE NOT DISPOSABLE COMMODITIES— THEY ARE OUR SONS AND DAUGHTERS

"The most important things in the world have been accomplished by people who have kept on trying when there seemed to be no hope at all."

~ DALE CARNEGIE ~

*E*AST HASTING AND MAIN STREET. SOMEONE LONG AGO CROSSED out the M in Main and put P in its place. And they were right. Unfortunately, all too many towns and cities have their skid row. Vancouver has a very large one.

This is an area of pain and suffering and human degradation, where I have watched addicts crawling on the sidewalk, searching for the tiniest bits of crack cocaine that someone may have dropped. Addicts picking scabs off their arms and smoking them for any bit of residual high they could get, sleeping in doorways or over grates, hoping to get a little bit of heat, with everything they owned in the shopping cart beside them.

People walk down the street, stepping over them, never really seeing the actual individuals there.

For God's sake, people, open your eyes. Please see, this is my son. This is someone's daughter. This woman has children in foster care, hoping that one day she will come and pick them up.

Addicts are not disposable commodities. They are our sons and daughters, and every one of them has someone, somewhere praying for them to come home. Crying themselves to sleep at night and, like me, asking God to keep an angel on their shoulder until they find their way.

~

Once again, Nathan was using very heavily, injecting heroin and cocaine all day, every day. He was living with his girlfriend of seven years.

Emelia was a lovely, kind, and gentle girl. Not a substance user or abuser, she was very much a lady. She was also extremely co-dependent, as was I for so many years.

So often, our wanting to help the addict becomes *our* addiction. Our very outlook on the day seems to depend on how the addict in our life is doing. If they are having a "good" day, so are we. When they are having a really bad time, our lives are devastated. That becomes our reality. We can't let go because that feels too much like abandonment when we are co-dependent.

~

Addicts go to unbelievable lengths. They really have a very distorted sense of reality.

I remember Nathan stole a necklace that Emelia's grandma had left to her. When Emelia confronted Nathan he of course denied it. Now the insanity of addiction is that even though he took and pawned the necklace, he spent the entire day turning her apartment upside down "trying to find it." His denial of the theft became an obsession almost to the point that he convinced himself he was trying to find it.

Somehow, that false reality also manifests itself in the "well, I'm not as bad as that guy" kind of thinking. The other guy's behavior is always worse. The addict will admit he has problems, but not like the other guy. "Hell, he's a fucking junkie."

Nathan has often said he didn't personally know anyone whose addiction was worse than his. At the same time, I overheard him and another addict mention being surprised as to what someone they knew would do to feed his addiction.

I overheard a fellow who was in a recovery program talking about how distorted an addict's sense of reality is. He recalled a time when it was cold and rainy, and he was homeless and huddled by a dumpster. However, he thought he was doing so much better than the guy behind another dumpster because, as he said, "At least I had a fucking lid on my dumpster and the other guy didn't."

Any addict in recovery would laugh at this story because they would all recognize themselves; that distorted reality was theirs too.

19

FROM 205 POUNDS TO 110 POUNDS
AND SEEING SNAKES EVERYWHERE

"Life consists not in holding good cards,
but in playing those you hold well."

~ AUTHOR UNKNOWN ~

SNAKES HAD ALWAYS BEEN NATHAN'S PHOBIA, HIS GREATEST fear. Even as a child, if he saw a picture of one in a book he commented that he didn't like them.

You may well have heard an expression, often in connection with alcoholics when they hallucinate, of a person "having the snakes." That is a very real and terrifying phenomenon. Often, the person will see creatures from a phobia, such as snakes or rats or spiders. In Nathan's case, it was snakes.

By this time, he was seeing snakes all the time—the carpets were snakes, snakes were coming out of the shower head and out of the toilet, snakes were in his clothes and on his body. He could not get away from them. You could see he was terrified all the time, though he tried to mask it. When feeling surrounded by such a visual hallucination all the time, it is very hard not to develop a strong paranoia.

Nathan's paranoia also put him on high alert. As on previous occasions,

he was sure policemen were following him everywhere, and was continually looking over his shoulder.

It was mid-December and his sister Jazz was home from Alberta for a few
days. Although Nathan often stayed away, by choice or necessity, he loved
his family and he loved Jazz. Knowing she was home, he came to see her. She
was shocked. Jazz had seen Nathan in bad states before but never like this.
He visited her for awhile and then asked for a ride back to the apartment.

When we dropped Nathan off, he gave Jazz a hug and said goodbye. She
was crying as she got back into the truck.

"I won't see Nathan again, will I Mom?"

"No baby girl, not unless we have a miracle."

We held each other and cried because we had no choice but to accept
that we were completely powerless, that we could not save Nathan from
himself.

Over the years, Jazz was understandably pretty tough with Nathan.
There were times when if he entered a room, she would walk out, or if he
asked a question, she would ignore him as if she hadn't heard. But for the
first time, she could not ignore that her brother was at a place where he was
dying. Where there may not be a tomorrow. Where there would just be
no more. She was heartbroken, and often angry with her brother, but she
always loved him. She always wanted better for him and better for all of us.

~

It was now two weeks later and Jazz was back in Alberta. It was also New
Year's Eve.

Nathan's arms had huge, open, weeping sores, necrotizing ulcers that
had developed from him injecting and then contracting infections. Some
were three inches long and two inches wide, and you could see the bone.
His arms were swollen two to three times their size from the infection, and
his normally 205-pound body was down to 110 pounds. He was 5 foot 10
inches tall and absolutely skeletal.

This son I loved so much was dying and I was powerless to save him.

I urged him to let me take him to the doctor, seeing he was at dire risk of losing his arms. He said, "Maybe tomorrow, Mom." But with an addict, tomorrow never comes.

Nathan's brother Michael and our friends, Jeff and Diane, together with Emelia and I, tried to convince Nathan to let us take him to the hospital. We talked to him and pleaded, but to no avail.

During our discussion, his cell phone rang. He excused himself, saying he had to meet a friend downstairs who had come by to pay him back $10 he had lent him.

I knew his dealer was making a delivery right to the apartment building. Nathan was worth big bucks to him. By this time, he had a $500 a day heroin and cocaine habit! The dealer knew full well that what he was delivering was killing my son, but that didn't matter. Until Nathan died, this guy knew he had a cash cow.

How do these people sleep at night? Where along the way did life come to mean so little to them? Where did they lose their souls?

Nathan had his fix and returned to the apartment, adamant that he would not go to the hospital that night but promising he would go at 10:00 the next morning.

Jeff, Diane, Michael, and I all hugged Emelia and Nathan. We told them we loved them, and I said I would be there at 10:00 a.m.

~

I thanked God that as another year was coming to an end, I still had my son, but for how long I didn't know. I actually asked God a favor that night.

"Please, God, if Nathan cannot find his way, please take him soon. He is suffering so very, very much. The thought that he would finally be safe, free, and in a peaceful place is the only thing that would make it okay. On every other level, it is an absolute tragedy. Take him to heaven, God; he has already lived in hell."

I could not bear the thought of losing my son, but given how horribly he was suffering, living seemed more cruel.

~

I looked back on that year, 2006. We'd had a lot of losses. My precious grandson Carlos was killed when he ran out from behind a car. It was eight days before his second birthday. I miss him every single day. I can still remember his little voice when I would call out to him, "Where are you, Carlos?"

"I coming, Nama."

"I love you, Carlos."

"I la lu Nama."

His death affected Nathan in a different way than the rest of us. We had all spent so much time with Carlos, and knew what made him so special. Nathan, though, because of his addiction, hadn't allowed himself to get close to Carlos, not really, and so his loss was one of never really knowing his nephew, and it affected him deeply.

~

My dad also died that year. We lost him and Carlos within two months of each other. Pop lived with us. He was 84 years old and we all loved him dearly. Nathan had tremendous love and respect for his Pop.

Michael had a group of friends over for his nineteenth birthday. Three were going to stay overnight. I had checked in on Pop about 10:00 p.m. and he was sleeping soundly. The kids were downstairs but they weren't overly noisy. All was quiet in the house by 2:00 a.m. and I went off to sleep.

At 4:00 in the morning, one of Michael's friends who had stayed over came running into my room yelling, "June, wake up, the house is full of smoke!"

My first thought was that someone had dropped a cigarette somewhere on the deck and it was smoldering. I yelled at all the kids to wake up, telling one to go upstairs quickly and tell Jazz and Michael to wake up. I told the others to get our two golden retrievers, Indy and Brandy, outside and call 911 immediately. Then I yelled at the first to come with me and help me get Pop up and outside.

I opened the door to Pop's bedroom and could not even see my hand in front of my face, the smoke was so thick. It was Pop's room that was on fire. I yelled at the kids to get the fire extinguisher and a pot of water. I could see Pop's bed in flames.

I crawled to the bed but Pop was not there. *Thank God*, I thought, *but where is he?* The lamp from his bedside table was on the bed. That's what started the fire.

The smoke was so thick I had to crawl on my hands and knees.

I finally found Pop on the floor. His eyes looked at me as if to say, "I knew you'd come but what the hell took you so long?"

By this time, Michael was flying down the stairs. He lifted Pop up off the floor and put him on a chair, then we wrapped a blanket around him and together carried him outside. We could hear the sirens getting closer. The firemen helped lift Pop into the ambulance.

The damage to his lungs was extensive. The following day, our family doctor ordered palliative care. Some of the family refused to believe that and told Pop he was looking good. But he knew he was dying. Pop only had a grade eight education, but he was a very smart man and very proud. He could read people probably better than anyone I've ever known.

Once, when everyone was out of the room, he said, "Juner, you've never lied to me and I don't want you to lie to me now. Am I dying?"

"Yes, Pop."

"Thank you for telling me the truth." And he was peaceful.

As drug-sick as Nathan was, he came for a few minutes every day to see Pop and tell him how much he loved him. We made a schedule so that at no time, even for a second, Pop would be alone. He had family around him every moment. Nathan took his turns sitting by Pop's bedside.

Within a couple of days, Pop was gone and we were devastated.

Nathan gave the eulogy at Pop's funeral, standing up and telling everyone how much Pop had meant to him. Pop would've been proud of him. I certainly was.

To some people, Nathan was "just a junkie." They didn't see the person or his pain, only the addiction.

Too many devastating losses. We all cope with loss in different ways. Nathan coped by losing himself, and he spiraled down very quickly.

~

So here it was, New Year's Eve. Michael and some friends were playing video games downstairs and I went up to bed. It had been a long day and I planned on being at Emelia's apartment the next morning at 10:00 sharp to take Nathan to the hospital. His arms really worried me. I had already seen people lose arms from staph infections. Nathan's arms were bad. *Really* bad.

At 1:00 a.m., the phone rang. Nathan was hysterical.

"There are bugs coming out of my arms! It's not the drugs playing with my mind, Mom. They are coming out of my arms. Come and get me to the hospital!" He wanted to go to the hospital across the street but I had other plans.

Our local hospital is not equipped to handle patients like Nathan. So many times in the past, he had gone to that emergency ward for help, but ours is a community of predominantly young families and senior citizens, not injection drug users.

St. Paul's Hospital in Vancouver was my choice. The staff there are amazing. They look after hard-core addicts every day, and they know what to do immediately. There is no mucking around, no judgment, just dealing with the immediate issue at hand. I knew that when we got there, the addiction wouldn't be a concern; saving his arms would.

I told Michael I was going to take Nathan into Vancouver.

"Mom, do you want me to come?"

"Please, Michael. I know I'll need help. I'm sorry."

Michael turned to his buddies and said, "Guys, here's my house key.

When you finish playing, just lock up the house and put the key through the mail slot. I'm going to help my mom with my brother."

When we arrived at the apartment block, Nathan was standing outside. It was cold and rainy. He had only his pants on—no shirt, jacket, shoes, or socks.

Michael got out and helped his brother into the back seat of the truck. Nathan was completely hysterical, pointing to his arms and yelling, "Look what's coming out of my arms! They're biting me!" He was screaming and crying at the same time. It was heart-wrenching.

Once Nathan was secured in the backseat, I turned left at the stop sign. Nathan yelled, "Go right. The hospital's right!'

"No, Nathan, we are going to St. Paul's."

He kept trying to crawl over the back of the seat and grab the steering wheel from me, but Michael did everything he could to keep him away so I could drive.

"Fuck you, Mom! Fuck you! You are fucking taking me hostage! Let me the fuck out of here. You fucking lied to me. I told you to take me to the hospital across the street."

"I didn't lie to you, Nathan. I said I would come and take you to the hospital, and I am. We have to go to St. Paul's. They can help you there."

"Fuck you! Fuck you! I fucking hate you! You fucking lied to me," all the while trying to get out of the truck or grab the steering wheel.

Michael was extraordinary. At one point he yelled back at Nathan, "No, Nathan, fuck you. Mom is trying to save your life. Now sit down and you shut the fuck up."

We didn't have a cell phone but at a red light a car pulled up alongside us. I rolled down my window and asked them if they had one. They said they did.

I asked them to take down my license plate number and call the police, to tell them that I was trying to get to St. Paul's Hospital in Vancouver, that my son was in a drug-induced psychosis and enraged. I asked them to ask the police if they would follow me in case I needed help, but to please not pull me over. I needed to get into the Vancouver municipality so that we could access the hospital there, not one en route.

It was the worst drive of my life. I was so afraid Nathan would be able to grab the steering wheel. Fortunately, it being New Year's Eve, the highway traffic was next to none. I don't think more than half a dozen cars passed us that night on the hour-long drive. An angel was on my shoulder and on Michael's that night.

I drove the entire way with my lights flashing. Only when I crossed the Oak Street Bridge and was in the Vancouver City limits did the police cruiser lights come on and the police pull me over.

Nathan tried to convince them he was fine and that he should be allowed to go, that we were overreacting. But they had already called for an ambulance to meet us; it arrived and took Nathan the rest of the way. I got back in the truck. My heart broke when I saw Michael crying. Nathan is thirteen years older than Michael, but tonight, like many times before and many times since, Michael had to step up to the plate and be the big brother. It was a heavy load. But he never wavered.

By the time the ambulance arrived at the hospital, the psychosis had subsided. The emergency room doctor looked at Nathan's arms and immediately scheduled him for the O.R.

While Nathan was undergoing the procedure, I returned to the truck in the underground parking garage to get my jacket. There was a knife and three syringes in the back seat. Nathan must have had them in his pants pocket.

What if he had thought Michael or I was a snake attacking him? In his psychosis, anything could have happened, and he would not even have been aware of reality. Thank you, God, that my Michael was not hurt and that we made it to the hospital safely.

They cleaned, debrided, and drained Nathan's arms. The E.R. doctor told Nathan he could have lost the one arm by morning and possibly the other as well. They put him on a strong regimen of antibiotics and instructions for follow-up.

I asked the doctor whether I could have Nathan held under the Mental

Health Act. He said no because Nathan wasn't battling mental illness psychosis, but rather drug-related psychosis. Two different conditions. Nathan was furious with me.

Hours later, Nathan was ready to go. He pulled his arms inside a t-shirt they had given him as we walked down the corridor of the hospital, toward the exit.

I saw a policeman sitting with a man in a wheelchair. The man had no legs. He was smiling and talking to himself, but you could make no sense of whatever it was he was saying.

I tried one more time, asking the policeman about the Mental Health Act; after all, my son was a danger to himself, was engaging in a form of self-murder. But the officer confirmed what the ER doctor had said.

He didn't stop there, though, and I will always be grateful. He said, "My name is Steve. I have been working the skids for a long time now, Nathan. I know when a man is dying, and Nathan, you are dying. You see this man sitting here?" and he pointed to the man in the wheelchair. "I bring him in here from time to time to get medical attention. One drug too many did this to him. He lost both his legs from injecting. A couple of years ago, he was walking around and could carry on a pretty intelligent conversation. Now he just sits and smiles and no one knows what he is trying to say. This could be you Nathan, very soon.

"There are 6,000 addicts in Vancouver and 3,000 of them have no home of their own. No one comes looking for them. It seems they have been given up on. But what I see here is that you have three people who love you and are begging you to get help. You have something that the 3,000 people down here don't have. Don't throw it away. Get help."

Then he shook Nathan's hand. I hugged the officer and left with Nathan.

His name, as he said, was Steve. I have never seen him again but he was a Vancouver Police Department officer on the Downtown Eastside and I will always be grateful to him for caring enough to talk to my son.

Thank you, Steve.

Four days later, Nathan went back into a detox facility.

20

THANK YOU TO ALL THE PEOPLE IN THE USA
WHO STEPPED UP AND GAVE US HELP

"If I have learned one thing in this life,
it is that God will not tie my shoes without me."

~ DOUG BOYD ~

OR YEARS NOW, NATHAN HAD FOLLOWED SO MANY 12-STEP programs, as well as gone to Narcotics Anonymous and Alcoholics Anonymous meetings. He'd been in and out of recovery houses and treatment centers, all based around the 12 steps. The 12-step programs work wonders worldwide for hundreds of thousands of people struggling with addiction. But it wasn't working for my son—or to put it another way, my son *wasn't working it.*

I started to wonder whether maybe it was time to try another avenue, so I went searching online. Narconon came up. Their program was different, and I thought that perhaps they could help Nathan. I called their 1-800 number. They had a program in Canada but they suggested that with Nathan's degree of addiction, he would be better to go to the program site in Louisiana.

One problem: Nathan was not allowed in the United States because he had drug convictions here in Canada on his record. But he seemed open to going to Narconon, and those of us who have loved ones struggling with addiction know that if there is that smallest interest in going to a treatment program, you have to jump at it before they change their minds. Often, the window of opportunity is miniscule.

I pulled up the acceptance letter from the facility and armed myself with every bit of information available on the web about their program. I had his birth certificate, driver's license, every piece of ID we thought might help, and we began our drive to the border, not sure of what would happen.

When we arrived, I told the guard that I was trying to get my son down to a treatment program. He asked Nathan whether he had ever been refused entry into the United States.

Nathan said he had.

So he gave us a slip and told us to go inside and wished us luck. I knew we were going to need it.

When we were called to the counter, I explained the situation—that we needed to get Nathan into the USA for this program, that we had tried many facilities before, but this one appeared different.

We spoke to several different officers. By this time I was exhausted and, try as I would, I could not stop the tears from flowing down my cheeks. I had run out of options and I was begging them to please let us into America.

I will never forget the kindness and compassion of those men at the border. They arranged a Humanitarian Waiver that would allow Nathan into the USA for three months to attend the program in Louisiana. If he was doing well after that time and it was felt he should remain longer, we could apply for an extension. We had spent several hours there, but we were now on our way.

Nathan wanted to stop for cigarettes but we were tight for time. I had checked all the flights leaving Seattle for Tampa, where Nathan would first go to a detox facility for ten days. From there he would go to Louisiana and the treatment center. I knew we had no more time to spare. Exiting the freeway for a cigarette run was out of the question. Nathan's mind and body was obviously craving the relief of pain heroin and cocaine would provide and now he was desperate for nicotine. So here we were driving down the I-5 to Seattle, desperate to use this window of opportunity with all his cravings and frustrations in high gear. It was a difficult drive for both of us.

But that is the world of addiction. Our adult children may be in their twenties or thirties, but their emotional growth is often stifled once their heavy drug use began.

If your child is like mine, that drug use likely planted its deep roots in the teen years, when so much is going on their minds and bodies. It is definitely a chaotic period in human life. Highs and lows, emotional upsets, high drama. And when they have addiction tendencies, they can become time-bombs.

We managed to arrive at the Seattle airport safely. I had never driven through Seattle before, let alone at night when street signs and stop lights seemed to come out of nowhere. It was a little daunting. But when it comes to using the almighty window of opportunity, nothing will stop us. It does not open often, and when it does, we will move heaven and earth to get our loved ones where they need to be. I ran ahead to see which airlines still had flights to Tampa.

~

Nathan had been on the methadone program here in British Columbia, where at certain approved pharmacies, heroin addicts can get a daily drink of methadone mixed in Tang to replace the heroin.

In total, Nathan was probably on the methadone program about five years. The first year was really good. He was no longer overdosing, and wasn't doing "the nod" continually, as heroin addicts do after fixing. For the first time in several years, he was able to work and function. I thought methadone was a miracle drug of sorts. But the only miracle will exist when a cure can be found for addiction.

My personal feeling about methadone is that it's like putting a Band-Aid on a gunshot wound. You are still a prisoner to the drug. One addiction is traded for another. Even if you are honest and faithful to the methadone program, you remain like a person handcuffed to a chair. You can stand up and stretch, but you can't walk away from the chair.

For many, the methadone program is a lifesaver. To Nathan, it became another on the list of those he was addicted to and could abuse. That was never his intention, but he was an addict and too often, that is what addicts do.

LSD, marijuana, mushrooms, heroin, cocaine, crack, Oxytocin, Demerol, morphine, Tylenol 3, Seroquel, Clonazepam, Ritalin, Percocet, Vicodin, ecstasy, methamphetamines—the list is endless. Smoked, crushed and snorted, injected—whatever is required to get the high, to escape.

They live this journey in a fog, a stupor, a false reality. Why?

We love them so much. We would do anything, give anything, take them anywhere required. But we have no control. Only that next fix has control, and we are powerless over it. All the love in the world cannot replace it. It becomes all-consuming to them: where to get the drug, then what to do to get it, use it, and then start all over again. It's a never-ending cycle.

~

So here we were at the Seattle airport. I started at the first flight counter in the long line of airline companies. I was hopeful; the terminal was still full of passengers, but it was now mere minutes before 10:00 p.m. I was panicking a little. If Seattle was like most Canadian airports, no flights went out after midnight.

The first three companies I checked with had either no flight going to Tampa or no seats available. The fourth company, thankfully, had two seats available. In first class!

What the hell. I had already remortgaged my house to the hilt, maxed out my credit cards, sold everything I could on Craigslist, and made every deal I could with God. Which credit card might have just enough left on it to pay for those first-class flights?

My plan had been to fly down there with Nathan, making sure he got where he was supposed to go. The detox clinic was sending personnel out to meet the flight. The cost was through the roof but the service was second to none, and the dedication and concern were exactly what we needed.

The cost of a first-class ticket made it impossible for me to buy a second ticket for myself. I had to trust Nathan would get there. He had to change aircrafts once. He assured me there would be no problem.

There wasn't.

The facility in Tampa called to confirm they had Nathan with them and were on their way to the clinic. I breathed a sigh of relief for the first time in ages, and prayed that this would be the miracle we were hoping for, that this would be the beginning of the end of Nathan's problems with addiction. I knew I had hit my rock bottom. I only hoped this was Nathan's as well.

He spent ten days at the detox centre in Tampa. They had medication there, not yet available in Canada, that he said made detoxing much more comfortable and manageable.

Nathan was now on the next leg of his journey, a flight from Tampa to Baton Rouge. The centre called when they had Nathan in their care. Once again, I breathed a sigh of relief.

~

Throughout the years of Nathan's addiction, he was grabbed off the street and held in various locations until drug debts were paid. He was beaten and brutalized, used and abused, had his hands smashed with hammers and guns shoved down his throat. He was beaten and tossed out of cars like a bag of garbage. But he is *not* garbage. He is my son.

~

Nathan and a couple of other guys all had drug debts that had gotten pretty high. They were grabbed and taken to a forested area, where one guy was hung up by his feet in a tree. A bonfire was started underneath. I can't imagine the fear and pain and screams before the fire was put out and he was cut down. They were told to do a smash-and-grab at a jewelry store to work off the debt. How would you ever get that image out of your head? A person cannot wake up from these nightmares.

~

We had a high-profile municipal politician in our community who developed an addiction to crack cocaine. He was doused with lighter fluid and set on fire because of an unpaid debt.

~

A mom I met had her home burned down because her son had an unpaid drug debt. She lost her home as a warning that the debt better be paid.

~

I also spoke to a mom whose son had some of his fingers cut off, then left in a box at her home as a threat: she had better come up with some money to pay her son's debt.

~

These are not television shows. They're real-life situations that happen far more often than anyone wants to believe. And they happen in our towns and cities, to our children.

These are truly evil, evil people, dealers and gang members who will go to any lengths to "collect" on unpaid debts. As parents of addicts, we know that every day reinforces that very real fear that it could be my son or your son or daughter today. We fear every day the lifestyle they are living, and we fear them dying. No one should live like that, and yet they continue the cycle.

If we can see it so clearly, why can't they?

What is missing?

We see people in every segment of society with addictions, those who were abandoned in childhood and those with strong, loving family bonds. We see people who were abused and others who were so loved and cherished. People from single-parent families, homes with both a mom and dad, overachievers and underachievers. People who grew up in poverty and those from affluent homes. Addiction knows no boundaries. Addiction is found in every possible category.

~

I should have known better than to get too comfortable when Nathan arrived in Louisiana. Five days after his arrival, I got a call that he was leaving the center.

The staff there was second to none. They had spent the last twenty-four hours trying to get Nathan to stay. We talked to him, pleaded with him to stay. We had an intervention of sorts on the phone. His sister Kiara talked to him and said she would fly down there to see him. Michael talked to him. We all begged Nathan to stay.

But he had made up his mind and was leaving. There was nothing and no one who could convince him to stay the course. He was an adult. They had no legal right to hold him after twenty-four hours, and I was responsible for flying him back home.

I had to arrange for a pre-paid ticket to be waiting for him at the airport. There was a first-class seat available on a flight that evening but the money was gone. I only had enough to pay for a cheaper seat on a flight the next morning.

When an addict decides to leave a place of help early, there is only one reason: he wants to use. My addict is no different than any other addict in that regard. He cashed in the airline ticket, went into Baton Rouge, rented a hotel room, and got high.

At 4:00 a.m., the phone beside my bed rang. I hadn't slept all night, just tossed and turned. I looked at the clock and knew it could only mean trouble.

The operator said I had a collect call from Nathan. As soon as I accepted the call, he blurted out, "Mom, I don't know what happened. I went for a walk and the next thing I knew, I woke up in a ravine. My shoes are gone, my pants are gone. They took my watch and St. Christopher medal, my wallet and all my ID. I'm freaking out. I don't even know where I am."

I told Nathan to call the center—they would come and get him.

The phone went dead.

I tried calling back the number on the call-display. It was a payphone and just rang and rang. I tried a dozen times, hoping someone would pick up. I didn't know whether pay phones in the USA accepted in-coming calls. Maybe it was like here in BC, where they don't.

I called the treatment center and told them what had happened. They said they would keep me posted if they heard anything from Nathan, and if they did, they would do everything they could to bring him back to the center. These people really cared.

I waited by the phone until morning, just praying that God would keep an angel on his shoulder and let me hear from him.

I was back and forth on the phone with Narconon all morning. Finally, I got a call from Jeanie. They had heard from Nathan. He wanted them to FedEx the money I had deposited in an account for him for incidentals during his stay there, to a hotel near the airport.

That was good news. They at least knew where he was. Jeanie told me she and another staff member would go to the hotel. She would have her cell phone with her and would call as soon as they made contact with Nathan. It was up to me to convince Nathan to go back with them.

They knocked on his hotel room door. Thinking it was FedEx, he opened it. Jeanie immediately handed Nathan the phone. "Nathan," I said, "you have no choice but to go back to the center. I have absolutely no way of getting you home. The money is gone, you have no ID, so you can't even board a flight, even if I did have the money. You have now lost your birth certificate, your driver's license, your social insurance card, your health care card, everything that says who you are. You have two choices. Go back to the center or be arrested, because that humanitarian waiver allowing you into the USA was only valid if you stayed at the center." He finally agreed to return, knowing his back was up against a wall.

The Narconon program incorporates hours of saunas to sweat the drug toxins out of the fat cells of the body. They claim the saunas, combined with megavitamins, oils, and proper nutrition, achieve this. That part of the program lasts approximately thirty days and then the classes begin.

Nathan called several times throughout that month and sounded so optimistic. He was singing the praises of the saunas and how much better he felt. He liked the people, and they did everything to make him feel comfortable. When he complained about his roommate, they gave him his own room. They were doing everything possible to insure he stayed. I felt he was on his way in a really positive direction.

Well, that was until the hard part began. A couple of days after the saunas were finished, so was Nathan. He called, saying he finally "got it" and was not staying there any longer. He was coming home.

I told him he had just finished the first part of the program. His future, clean and sober, depended on him learning the rest of the program. Living clean and sober, for someone who never has, would be a daunting experience. He needed to learn the tools for problem solving, anger management, and personal planning. The first part of the program cleaned his mind and body so that he could absorb the skills necessary to live a full and productive life, drug free.

We pleaded with him again to stay. Kiara did. Michael did. I did. The center did. He would not budge.

~ 21 ~

THE DAY THINGS CHANGED

"You have all the tools and resources you need.
What you do with them is up to you.
Take responsibility for yourself.
Learn to let go when you cannot change things."

~ CHERIE CARTER-SCOTT ~

THAT WAS THE DAY WHEN SOMETHING IN ME CHANGED. Part of me blamed myself for Nathan's addiction. If you're a parent, you probably have blamed yourself on some level as well. That's what we parents do. After all, if we were doing such a good job at raising our children, how could something be so wrong?

And of course, it's not just parents who suffer doubt and guilt. "If I were such a good sister/brother/husband/wife/partner/friend/other, why couldn't I stop this person I love so much from using?"

I had always tried to understand addiction as being a disease, and to apply the appropriate logic:

If all you had to do to stop cancer was to stop drinking coffee, you would stop in a heartbeat. If all you had to do to stop the progression of MS or Alzheimer's or some other awful disease was to sit in the sunlight for four hours a day, everyone would do that. So why then would an addict continue on this journey to hell if all he or she had to do was stop?

But it obviously isn't that easy, otherwise there would be no addicts.

Nevertheless—I had had enough. By that time, I had spent sixteen years doing absolutely everything I could. My bank account was empty. My home was mortgaged to the hilt. My credit cards were maxed out. I was in my fifties, had worked since I was eight years old, and for the last twenty years had worked sixty hours a week, and I couldn't even afford a vacation.

I had made sure Nathan had access to the best treatment centers in our area. I visited him every week. I made sure he had money for incidentals and new clothes each time he entered a facility, so he felt better about his appearance. I encouraged and loved him unconditionally. I was there to catch him every time he fell and to help him back up. *That was perhaps the biggest problem. That was my biggest mistake.*

I hadn't had a full night's sleep in over sixteen years. His addiction had made me ill.

I was tired.

~

And now, here he was in beautiful Louisiana, ready to run.

I tried everything, including bribery. I told him if he finished the program and stayed until they said he was good to go, I would somehow find a way to help him pay off his debts and get him a new start. I would help him in every way possible.

But I refused to buy him a return ticket home this time, because he needed to be there at the center. His life depended on it. I told him that if he left, *there was no more*, that he would not be able to live at home. I would provide neither shelter, nor food, nor clothing—nothing.

So, he sold his iPod, his cell phone, and everything else he needed to get the money for a Greyhound ticket back to Canada. At that time, he didn't need ID to take the bus.

When in Dallas, he was arrested and spent the night in jail for being intoxicated. Where he ever got the idea that he was ready to leave the center is beyond me; less than three hours after leaving Louisiana, he was in trouble. The authorities released him with a summons, on the promise he would appear in court at the end of August, and sent him on his way.

He got on another Greyhound and continued the ride up to the USA/ Canada border, getting off in Blaine, Washington, where he called and asked me to pick him up.

Up to that point, I had rarely said no to anyone. But this was not the old me. Something in me changed the day Nathan called from Louisiana. For perhaps the first time in my entire life, I found my power. I finally realized that *no one can use me if I don't allow it.*

I didn't question myself this time. I knew a different approach was imperative. Nothing I or anyone else had done in the past had helped Nathan stay clean and sober. I had to accept that sometimes, helping hurts, whereas rescuing only prolongs—that sometimes, kindness kills. I had to stop the Mr. Nice Guy routine if I were to have a hope in hell of saving my son, and this had to be an all or nothing decision, otherwise it would definitely be only a matter of time before he was dead.

So, I refused to pick him up.

He managed to get a ride from someone else and the next day turned up at our home. I told him he could not stay with us and there was no help for him here; he had burned that bridge when he decided to leave the treatment centre again. I told him that if he would let me take him back to treatment, the help and support would be there—otherwise, he was on his own.

His comment was, "Fine, thanks for nothing."

His car was parked in the driveway but it wasn't licensed or insured. I knew he would be back for it as soon as he could steal a license plate, which didn't take long. The battery was dead, so he pushed it out of the driveway, onto the road, and a neighbor across the street gave his battery a boost. He squealed the tires to let me know he was pissed off. I made no attempt to talk to him further.

Nathan had burned pretty much every bridge around, so I knew he would end up sleeping in his car.

In spite of his lifestyle, Nathan liked to be clean, shaved, and presentable. Whenever he lived at home, he showered daily, sometimes twice, and wore clean socks, underwear, and shirt every day. Maybe he would wear his jeans two days, but never more than that. Sleeping in his car was not going to cut it for Nathan now that he had been off the street and in good accommodations for awhile.

Nathan showed up at the house again two days later, looking pretty bedraggled, and said he was hungry. I asked him whether he was willing to go back to the treatment centre in Louisiana, pointing out that I had paid for very comfortable accommodations for him there, and they were willing to take him back one more time.

He refused.

I went to the kitchen, came back with a loaf of bread and a jar of peanut butter, and said, "Make it last." That was clearly not the response Nathan had been counting on.

I love my son so deeply. To put up this wall was not easy; I knew he felt rejected and that bothered me. He had so many times over the years felt rejection, but never from me. It broke my heart to hurt his feelings, yet I had finally come to the realization that our mutual foe did not battle on a level playing field. Addiction was holding my son hostage and killing him in the process. He was still powerless over the drug, but I couldn't be.

The next day, Nathan came back to the house and said he obviously had no option but to go back. I thought, *Thank you, God.* When I called the treatment center in Louisiana, they confirmed they would take him back this one last time.

~

We now had a major hurdle to overcome: Nathan still had no ID. This was going to be a real problem. Since the horrific September 11 attacks on the United States in 2001, the rules for crossing the border had become rigid, and ID was absolutely necessary.

Not only was I going to be asking the border service to let Nathan, despite his criminal record, over one more time, but I also had no official documents to verify his identity.

I pulled out every report card from kindergarten on up, as well as his baptismal, first communion, and confirmation certificates. I took all his Red Cross swimming tests paperwork, and all his elementary and high school report cards, as well as photo albums. One way or another, I had to prove he was my son Nathan, and convince the authorities once again of why we wanted to go to the USA.

I pulled up to the border, described our circumstances to the border guard, and as before, was handed a slip of paper and directed inside. While waiting to be called, I was praying. When it was our turn, we approached the desk. I explained the whole situation and they pulled up Nathan's name in the computer. The overnight jail stay in Texas came up, and it looked like things might be over right then and there.

"Tell me, sir—why should we allow you back into our country? We have enough of our own criminals down here. Why would we want to take Canadian criminals as well?"

Nathan just shrugged his shoulders. He didn't want to be there in the first place and would have been quite happy if they had turned us back. Then it would have been the border guard's "fault" rather than his.

I pulled out all the report cards and certificates I had brought with me. They could clearly see that this was an act of a desperate mother, that I had nothing left. At that point, they took Nathan for finger-printing, as they had done the previous time.

The officer in charge was stern with Nathan. "Why would you leave in the first place? We already gave you a humanitarian waiver. You obviously didn't take this as seriously as you should have. That was a privilege, not a right. Go back and sit down."

They were clearly frustrated and disgusted, and understandably so. I was beginning to hold out very little hope, so I just kept praying.

Finally an officer called me up to the desk. Then he called Nathan. "There is only one reason we are letting you through: your mother. I'll tell you straight up—if you were my brother, I'd kick your ass right into the hospital for what you are putting her through, not into another treatment center. Get out of here. This is your last chance."

Once again, we were on the I-5, heading south to the Seattle Airport. When we arrived we should have been running to the counter but Nathan stopped, determined to have a cigarette before entering the terminal building. He sure had no intention of making it easy.

Once at the counter, we asked about a flight to Baton Rouge, but this time it could not be via Dallas because of the outstanding criminal charge from his previous trip. I purchased a ticket and Nathan headed for security, again getting pulled over for a secondary search because his criminal record meant his name was flagged.

I waited about an hour and then approached the counter, needing to put my mind at ease and verify he was on the aircraft before I headed back north to Canada. Explaining the situation, I asked the counter attendant whether Nathan had boarded his flight.

"Sorry, not yet. Passengers have already boarded but it will be a couple more minutes before the doors close. Check back with me in five."

Five minutes seemed like five hours. Where could he be and why hadn't he boarded?

I approached the counter once more. "I'm sorry, ma'am, your son did not show up at the gate. Boarding is finished and the aircraft door has now closed."

My heart was racing. I felt nauseous and faint, and tears were streaming down my face. For that moment, I felt like the bottom had completely fallen out of my world.

Calm, June. Breathe. It's not over. Think. Think. What's the next step?

Here I was in a huge airport, unfamiliar with the rules and regulations of the FAA or with the laws of the USA.

I asked whether there was any way of getting some sort of pass so that I could go through security and try to find Nathan. The airline counter attendant was sympathetic and called her supervisor. They issued me a pass.

~

I have to digress for a moment and say that I thoroughly appreciate, from the bottom of my heart, the United States of America. At every roadblock I encountered along the way, some very helpful and considerate person in a position of authority stepped up to the plate and did everything he or she was legally able to do to help me get my son where he needed to be. This is a compassionate country, a country where I found people went the extra mile. I will never forget the kindness and consideration we received, or a single face of those who helped on our journey. Each and every one will remain in my heart forever.

~

I checked each gate along the way and every men's bathroom—yes, I did that! There was still no sign of Nathan. Then, just as I was about to turn back and retrace my steps, I saw him sauntering by. Relief flooded over me.

"Nathan, where have you been? Why did you miss your plane? What's going on?"

"Just go home, Mom. I registered for the next flight. It's no big deal."

No big deal? Wrong. This was a very big deal to me.

"But why did you miss your plane? You had plenty of time to get to the gate."

"Go home and leave me alone. I don't want to be going there but I am.

So leave me the fuck alone and go home." He then turned and strode away as quickly as he could, determined to get away from me, and sat tucked away in an area where he got the last available seat.

Understand—this was not my son being disrespectful, and I didn't take it personally. The addict was fighting this trip every step of the way. My son Nathan wasn't angry at me. My son the addict was. That is a huge difference. Only those of us who love an addict can relate.

Well, I had come this far and I'd be damned if I was going to leave before I saw him board that aircraft, so I plunked myself down in the seat closest to the boarding gate and sat there for an hour and a half before boarding began.

By this time I was physically and emotionally exhausted. If all had gone as planned, I should have been getting close to the border, about an hour away from my comfortable, warm bed. Instead, I was trying to stay awake, watching Nathan, the addict, glaring at me from across the room.

Finally, it was his time to board. He walked right by me without saying a word.

I said, "Good luck, sweetie, I love you," then picked up my backpack and headed out of the terminal, stopping only to thank the girl who had spoken to her supervisor about getting me a pass to find Nathan.

By now it was 1:00 a.m. I found my truck in the parking arcade, followed the direction of the exit sign, and began heading north. It was just after 4:00 a.m. when I got to the border. There were no other vehicles in front of me or pulling in behind me, and only two gates were open. I pulled in to the gate on the left.

The Canada border guard was friendly. "Late night. Where you coming from?"

I guess all I needed was a friendly face and a kind voice. I started crying and blurting out every detail of the last twelve hours. The poor guy, he just wanted to know where I was coming from. I think he was a little blind-sided. But one thing was certain—within a few minutes, he absolutely understood where I was really coming from.

"You get on home now and, um, best of luck."

I pulled into my driveway and walked into the house. My two golden retrievers, Indy and Brandy, were there with their tails wagging. Their unconditional love has gotten me through many difficult days over the years.

Michael had dozed off in a chair downstairs by the door, waiting for me to get home. He opened his eyes. "How'd it go, Mom?"

"Just fine, Pal." (That's Michael's nickname.) "You go upstairs and get some sleep now."

My workday starts at 6:00 a.m. There was just enough time to shower and "put on the happy." We may be heartbroken and crumbling on the inside, but the outside world doesn't stop for heartbreak. Somehow, we get through another day because there is no choice.

~

Midway through the day, I got a call. Nathan had safely arrived at the centre. Seventy-two hours later, Nathan was asked to leave. He was being disruptive, disrespectful, and problematic to the others, who were working hard on their program.

He had already decided he didn't want to be there. Nothing and no one could have made it work. Nathan was in a fight with the devil, and right now the devil had won yet another round.

I got a call from Jeff, one of the counselors. Nathan had been taken to the airport and he was on his way back to Canada; the center had paid for the ticket. Jeff said he had had, "a lot of tough nuts to crack, but not one as tough as Nathan." He was genuinely sorry and wished me the best before saying goodbye.

They had gone above and beyond what I had ever expected, and I will forever be grateful for their support and effort. They were all truly caring people.

~ 22 ~

HOLDING ONTO OUR POWER . . .
AND LETTING GO

*"Do what you can, but never forget that letting go
is very different from giving up. Of all the things you can make in life,
remember you make all the difference in your life."*

~ AUTHOR UNKNOWN ~

*I*F NOTHING ELSE IN MY JOURNEY RESONATES WITH YOU, *please* read and reread this chapter as many times as you have to—nothing will be as important as these thoughts. Your child's life depends on this, as sure as I am a mom. It took me far too long to finally realize this in my heart. There is a reason for the phrase "tough love." Nothing will be harder, but nothing will make more of a difference than your actions. In the case of addiction, loving and understanding and helping hurts the addicts we love and can ultimately lead to their deaths.

~

I had tried every day for sixteen years to save this son I love so much. Nathan's brother and sisters had tried. Nathan had tried; he really had.

Could tough love earlier have made Nathan's journey any harder? *Absolutely not.* His journey has been horrific for him. We will never know whether he could have stopped sooner or would have died. But I cannot imagine that he or anyone could have had a tougher road than the one that took him to the bowels of hell, to places and people you only dream of in your worst nightmares.

He overdosed several times on city sidewalks. He endured abuses that left me curled in a ball, sobbing, because I had to come to terms with the fact that I had no power to stop him, no power to save him. Only he had the power.

I wish I had made it so difficult that he may have hit his bottom years earlier, but I always rescued him, thinking *that* was what it meant to love him.

Then I finally came to a place, an epiphany if you will, where I said:

"I recognize your right to make your own decisions, even though they are so wrong and damaging. But while I respect your right, I also respect myself enough to know that I do not now, never have, and never will condone drug use, and I will not be a part of keeping you where you are for one more day.

"From this day on, I will not pay your bus fare. I will not buy you groceries. I will not run every time there is an emergency. I have sat by your side in emergency rooms and hospital rooms and treatment centers and court hearings. Today this stops.

"Everything a good parent should do, I have done, and more. Let me know when you are ready to help yourself, and show yourself and your family the respect and consideration we all deserve. I can't help you if you are not ready and willing to help yourself. You want to make all the choices and be protected from all the consequences. Life does not work that way.

"If you want to be the best you can be, let me know and I will help you every step of the way. Until then, there is nothing more I will do, because to give you what you want keeps you just comfortable enough to keep you where you are."

Saying something like this entails going against everything we have ever felt that it means to love someone, but in the end it may be the only way to stop the insanity that is drug addiction. For me, nothing else had worked.

If we continually run to the rescue, they don't have to make any changes. Inadvertently, we are telling them, "Don't worry, I'll catch you every time." I did this for so many years. And I was wrong.

Our kindness and understanding conveys that "it'll be okay." But it *isn't* okay, because they are living in a manner that destroys them and others. Despite our best intentions, the desire to "understand" becomes a ticking time bomb. By constantly rescuing and helping, we send the message that they really don't have to make any changes. Consequently, we are the ones making all the compromises.

Changing our approach doesn't happen overnight, and they will fight us all the way in whatever way they have learned works. At some point, though, we have to stand firm, even while we second-guess our every decision—I certainly did.

Will they fall down more quickly without our help? Yes. But they may realize sooner rather than later that life as they have known it has changed. The emotional price of their addiction is just too high.

The path does deteriorate before it starts to improve, and you have to be prepared for their journey to take you to places of unbearable pain as you watch and have to stand back. Yet only they have the power to stop this madness. No one can walk this horrific journey for them.

I know you will feel lost. But you have already lost yourself, because absolutely every waking moment of every day seems consumed with "What did I do wrong? What shouldn't I do? How can I help? How can I keep from making things worse?" You are constantly thinking that it must be something you have some control over. *You don't.* Being understanding and making excuses and helping only prolongs the pain and suffering for you, and even more so for them.

So have we failed our loved ones? No, I do not believe we have. We must give ourselves a little bit of compassion here, a little bit of self-love. We have done the best we could with what we believed was the right thing. But we have been fighting a disease that doesn't play by any rules.

Failure occurs only when you refuse to address a situation. We don't learn lessons by all the things that go right. The greatest lessons we learn are from our mistakes. Falling down isn't a failure, but staying down is—so when you fall in the water, get out before you drown. They will test everything you are, and just when you think you can't face another situation, something else will come up, and you know what? *You'll face it.* You may well face it differently, but you will face it.

We have to say and mean it: "You may have decided the way you will continue to allow your life to go, but I do not give you permission, not one more day, to take me down with you." And stand firm. If you waiver, even slightly, it is only a matter of time before your addicted loved one becomes the puppet master again. That sounds harsh, I know, and it's heartbreaking to hear, because our love is so deep. But as much as the addicted person loves us, he loves the high more. We will always take a back seat to the addiction.

So, at some point, enough has to be enough.

The most important thing to remember is to stand firm on what you feel, to stand firm on what you know is right. Say what you mean and mean what you say. No more lines in the sand that are continually washed away by the waves. Carve those lines in stone. When we fail to stand firm in what we believe, we will find ourselves falling for anything.

I fully and painfully realize that this isn't easy, especially as our addicts are masters at the art of manipulation. It is the only way they can continue. Still, ask yourself: how many times did you drive your addicted loved one to his dealer because he was so sick that he needed "help" just to get through the night? "Tomorrow, I promise, I'll quit."

How many times have you given your addicted loved one money because he didn't make it to the pharmacy to get his methadone and is in so much pain? He's crying, retching, doubled over. But he can buy some methadone from a guy he knows. I have. You give him a ride but he says you have to park down the street. He'll be right back.

Why did we do this? Because we believed them.

We changed the bearing of our moral compass to accommodate what we needed to believe—that this really was the very last time. But of course, it wasn't. We told ourselves we would never stand being used again. Yet we were.

~

I always had real difficulty in mentally and emotionally separating "letting go" from "abandonment." I could never abandon my children. I could never abandon Nathan. I could never give up on him. But I finally realized I *had* to "let go."

There is a crucial difference between giving up and letting go. *Letting go* means we recognize that we cannot change the behavior and can no longer live with it. So, we give it to the God of our understanding, whether that be God in heaven, the universe, or our angel. Say to yourself: "I have not given up. No, never. I have just had to let go. There is something he needs to learn and I will never understand it. I have tried everything I can to help and I cannot stop it. So I give him his space, as I accept that I cannot walk beside him right now, but I will always be there when he is ready."

It has to be all or nothing. Partway doesn't work, because it gives the addict the feeling that he still has a foot in the door. It has to be: "No, I will not buy you new shoes, jeans, jacket, or mitts." When he ends up back in hospital or court or jail and expects you to be there to visit, don't. The action you take or don't take has to shake him to his core.

He will expect you to waiver—you always have. Now is the time to dig in your heels, because you *will feel guilty* and you will say to yourself, "Just this last time." That is all it takes for you to lose some control again, and then you are back at square one; you have again given the addict the control.

All this sounds horrific and mean, and you will definitely feel that way. But nothing you have done so far has changed the situation, so you have to take a whole new path. He will go downhill. That is a given. The hope, though, is that he will reach back up because he has no choice, and then, just maybe, it can be the start of rebuilding.

Your addict will hate you. At least, that is how he will make you feel. Just remember, it is not your loved one who hates you in reality. It is the addict within.

What choice have you been given? You have no control at all and yet you want to save this person whom you love so much. You have to get to a place where you get your power back, and that means *letting go* of the addict.

Things can't stay the status quo. It's not working. It never has and it never will. Don't wait until further damage occurs—and it will. The longer you wait, the farther he'll fall and the harder it will be to get him back.

~

A brief word here about anger.

Something so very important, and something that I still have not been able to implement, is: *It's healthy to get angry.* Everything in me, everything anyone has ever told me, everything I have ever read, indicates that it is healthy to get angry. I have to admit that in that sense, I am not healthy yet. Why? I don't know, I only know that I do not possess the emotion "anger." It is a reality I have lived with my entire life.

I feel disappointment. I feel sadness. I feel hurt. I feel happiness and joy-fulness. I feel hope and thankfulness. When I see injustice or intolerance against another person, I immediately step in and say it is unacceptable. But I do not feel anger. So my journey to "getting healthy" is still a work in progress. That said, although I do not get angry, I have definitely learned to say, "*Enough is enough*," and mean it.

I mention this because it may also be difficult for you to feel anger. *But you can still draw the line and insist that you've had enough.*

~

I had told Nathan that if he came back without finishing the program, there would be no help from me.

He told me there were no more programs, recovery houses, or treatment centers he was willing to go to. He said he "got it," and never again would go into a program—he had heard the program a thousand times, he had done the steps, and that was it. There was nothing else he could learn from them. He said we had to trust that he knew what he was doing.

Well, I had reached my bottom. Not because I was giving up. No, never. But I knew there was nothing else I could do. I had tried everything, given— and given up—everything.

A key slogan in Al-Anon and Nar-Anon is "Let go and let God."

I'd had to let go, and now I had to "let God."

The most difficult thing for the parent or the loved one of an addict to do is step back and watch where the chips may fall—knowing full well they almost certainly will not be in a good place.

~ 23 ~

HOW DO ALL THE DRUGS
GET INTO NORTH AMERICA?

*"You are not a victim of fate or circumstances.
Things happen to you because of how you are and what you do."*

~ C. CARTER-SCOTT ~

*T*HE DRUG TRAFFICKERS AND IMPORTERS, THOSE WHO LIVE
in the mansions on the hill with the five-car garages and living
rooms that overlook the lights of the city, the designer kitchens and huge
sunken bathtubs—they have the lifestyle that you and I, the honest, hard-
working people, will never see. But we earn our paychecks by honest work
and honest living. At the end of the day, we may sink our tired bodies into
a bathtub not large enough to stretch out in, but we haven't destroyed anyone's life to get that bathtub, either. So, we sink down in the warm water,
and for a couple of minutes we try to forget.

~

How *does* all that cocaine and heroin get into North America?

For all the shipments that get caught on container ships, at airports, at all the points of entry, so many slip by. This is not because someone is lax on the job; it is just that these people smuggle using every conceivable method, often in ways that are nearly impossible to detect. Obviously, not every single item on a ship can be checked every single time.

The drugs arrive inside soccer balls and basketballs made by companies overseas that in reality are owned or paid off by the very people living in the mansions, who never seem to get their hands dirty. They have other people to do that.

The drugs are sewn inside the lining of a shipment of leather jackets, bound for a high-end store. Maybe in the hems of skirts. Hidden inside pottery or amongst shipments of fruit and vegetables. Or strapped to a "mule"—your loved one or mine, who has a drug debt to work off.

Hockey bags stuffed full are carried in the dark of night, through the snow, in an area of the USA/Canada border they figure isn't on the radar. If they get caught, that's the risk and cost of doing business.

Unknowingly, we help to launder money. The grocery store where we buy our milk and bread. The garage where we get our car serviced. The high-end vehicle import business. The motorcycle shop. The race track. The fitness gym. The casino. The land developer. The lawyer. The import business. The shop selling diesel generators or grain harvesters. Most are honest companies. But tucked in alongside the honest ones are these businesses who front the drug trade, who launder money. They're disguised as legitimate companies, doing business with us every day. Unknowingly, we help them launder their dirty money with our hard-earned paychecks.

~ 24 ~

SCREWED AGAIN

"Some days, doing 'the best we can' may still fall short
of what we would like to be able to do, but life isn't perfect on any front,
and doing what we can with what we have
is the most we should expect of ourselves or anyone else."

~ MISTER ROGERS ~

TOUGH LOVE IS HARD ON THE ADDICT AND HARD ON THOSE who love the addict.

Would I "let go" if Nathan were struggling with leukemia or bone cancer? Would I "let go" if he were dying of AIDS? No. I would do everything possible to make him comfortable and tend to his needs every day, all day, for however long was necessary.

But addiction is unlike what we most often consider a disease. In my opinion, it is in a category all its own. Why? Because with addiction, when we help the addict and keep him comfortable, we help in the escalation of his disease. I believe that is why it often takes us so long to come to terms with addiction and how best to go through that journey.

Tough love. This was the only choice I had left. To love my son, I had to let him fall, and fall he would. I knew this.

If there is one thing Nathan needs, it's his family. He loves his family. Yes, he loves drugs more. That's a no-brainer to anyone who knows and loves an addict. But love us he does. To have us pull away from him would put him on a downward spiral and I knew it. He would go downhill fast. Yet we had run out of options. He had to finally hit bottom, and I no longer had any delusion as to how far down he might have to go to find that bottom, if there even was one for him to hit.

I had told Nathan that if he did not complete the program in Louisiana, he would no longer receive any help from me. I knew I could not budge. If I were to waiver, Nathan would know that it was business as usual with me, that no matter what he did or where he had fallen to, Mom would be there to pick him up, dust him off, get him cleaned up for just long enough to feel healthy again, and out he would go. The call of heroin, the call of cocaine, was like a dangerous and passionate love affair that he could not resist.

His car had been impounded for being on the road uninsured and with a stolen license plate, so he no longer had that to sleep in. Over the next two weeks he lived on the street or occasionally couch surfed. He looked terrible, and when I saw him, my heart ached.

I had a spare bedroom at home. I had a refrigerator with food in it. I gave to the food bank. How could I convince myself that to leave him on the street would help him? *That* was love? It sure didn't feel like love to me. It was all I could do to walk away.

Two weeks later, he came by the house, saying he couldn't get a job if he didn't have a place to live, a place to sleep and clean up. He had met a guy at an AA meeting who had a furnished spare bedroom and was willing to rent it to him for $375 a month. He would also have to give a damage deposit of $187.50.

Nathan told me he had talked to his old boss in construction and he could go back to work for him. "Could you just help me this one last time, Mom? I can't get off the street if I don't have a job, and I can't get a job if I have no place to live."

He was right.

I wrote a check for the damage deposit; I wouldn't have the $375 until I got paid in a couple of days. Could he explain to the guy that I would give him the rent then?

Nathan said that would not likely be a problem. He could probably move in, now that at least he could give the guy the damage deposit and the promise of payment for the month in just a couple of days.

~

Nathan has pretty much always worked in the construction industry, except for a few jobs in the food industry. I don't know how many hard hats, rain suits, and steel-toed boots I have bought him through the years; pretty much enough to start up a small store, I would imagine. But he would need those articles if he was going to start working. Plus, it was getting cold now and soon we would be in our winter season.

Once again, I pulled out my credit card, picked up rain gear, a hard hat, a lined red-plaid jacket, some gloves, and a pair of steel-toed boots. I stopped by the grocery store and picked up enough luncheon meat and bread so he could make sandwiches for the week to take to work, and a one-week booklet of bus tickets for his transportation to and from the site. I went to the place Nathan was staying, stopping only long enough to drop off the purchases, give him a hug, and tell him I loved him. He was genuinely grateful.

Two days later, I gave him $375 to pay his landlord.

~

A couple of days passed. I had not heard from Nathan so I was confident he was working and doing as well as could be expected. I then had a call. Could I meet him? I agreed.

Our friends Jeff and Diane were over for dinner that evening and Diane offered to drive me. She loves Nathan and wanted to see him as well.

When we met up with him, he looked terrible. He was sketchy and clearly using. Tired and drawn, he asked for more bus tickets and wondered whether I could buy him a prepaid grocery card. He should still have had two days of tickets left, but he explained that he had traded them with a guy at work for some food.

That could have been true.

I went into the store and bought another book of tickets but only pulled out one day's worth. He asked several times for me to give him the whole book. "This is ridiculous. Just give me the book of tickets."

"No, Nathan. I will meet you each day and give you a day's worth. And no, I will not buy you a grocery card, but I will take you inside and get you some groceries."

"This is bullshit," he said and walked away.

No, this is drug addiction. I knew that he wanted the book of bus tickets and the grocery card to sell or trade for drugs.

My heart broke for my son. He did not want to be an addict. Nobody does. But for whatever reason, he just did not know how to get out of it.

The next day, I went by the house where he was renting the room. The landlord said he hadn't seen him for three days and he was angry because Nathan owed him rent.

"His rent is paid up, isn't it?"

"The only money I've gotten from him is the check from you for the damage deposit. He said you were going to pay the rent, but I haven't seen it."

"But I gave him $375 to give you."

"Lady, your son is a crackhead. I haven't seen him in three days. When he is here, he sleeps all day in his room."

"He told me he got a job at a construction site in the city."

"Well, not unless the job starts at three in the afternoon he doesn't. I'm sorry, lady, but he has to go. I have all his things in a garbage bag in the garage. Could you take them with you?"

~

Fewer than twenty hours later, I had a call from Nathan. "Has anyone been looking for me? Has anyone called or stopped by?"

"Who is supposedly looking for you, Nathan?"

"Sorry, gotta go."

I was worried. I had no idea who might be looking for Nathan or what the fallout could be. He was going down fast, as I knew he would, and I could not stop the downward spiral. It had to happen. I only hoped he would reach out for help before he died.

At this point, I had to again accept that Nathan could be nearing death, either by a dealer or from the drugs. He was very sick. Addiction had racked every fiber of his being. It had a power over him that was unimaginable, as strong as the pull of a mother for her child.

"Hit that bottom and ask for help, Nathan. I cannot bear to lose you. I love you, my son, more than you could ever imagine."

~ 25 ~

POLITE ROBBER HITS BANK

"Without self-discipline, success is impossible, period."

~ LOU HOLTZ ~

THE LOCAL NEWSPAPER ARRIVED. I DIDN'T USUALLY LOOK AT it while I was working, but I had a few minutes so I thumbed through the first couple of pages.

A headline hit me. "Bank Robber Described As Calm, Polite."

A chill ran through me. Nathan is generally very polite in dealing with people. He always has been. Even in some of his worst moments, he was usually polite and very likeable.

I picked up the paper and sat down, knowing before even reading the article that it was Nathan. The article said the robber was very polite, wore a red-plaid jacket, and carried a hard hat.

Nathan had a $500-a-day heroin and cocaine addiction. That is $15,000 a month. Virtually no one can afford to support a hardcore addiction legally; you have to do a lot of crime to pay for it.

Not five minutes later, I received another call from Nathan. "Has anyone called looking for me, Mom?"

"Nathan, are we talking about the police or a bad guy? I need to know."

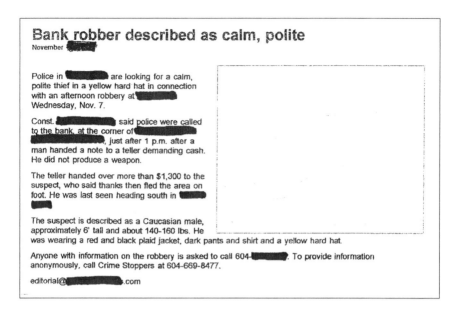

Bank robber described as calm, polite

November ▮▮▮▮

Police in ▮▮▮▮▮▮▮ are looking for a calm, polite thief in a yellow hard hat in connection with an afternoon robbery at ▮▮▮▮▮▮▮ Wednesday, Nov. 7.

Const. ▮▮▮▮▮▮▮▮ said police were called to the bank at the corner of ▮▮▮▮▮▮▮ ▮▮▮▮▮▮▮▮▮, just after 1 p.m. after a man handed a note to a teller demanding cash. He did not produce a weapon.

The teller handed over more than $1,300 to the suspect, who said thanks then fled the area on foot. He was last seen heading south in ▮▮▮▮ ▮▮▮

The suspect is described as a Caucasian male, approximately 6' tall and about 140-160 lbs. He was wearing a red and black plaid jacket, dark pants and shirt and a yellow hard hat.

Anyone with information on the robbery is asked to call 604-▮▮▮▮▮▮. To provide information anonymously, call Crime Stoppers at 604-669-8477.

editorial@▮▮▮▮▮▮▮.com

"Have the police been there looking for me?"

"No, Nathan, no one's been here, but I have to know. I just read the newspaper. Did you rob a bank?"

"Yes. I was desperate. I owed a guy and if I didn't pay, I was a dead man."

"Okay, Nathan, now you've put me in the position where I have to turn you in. You know that, don't you?"

"Mom, I'm in detox right now. I want to finish detox and then turn myself in. Can you just sit on this until I finish detoxing? I promise, I'll turn myself in. I need to."

"Okay, Nathan. I'll wait. But you make sure you finish detoxing, and I'll go with you to turn yourself in."

"Thanks, Mom. I love you."

"I love you more."

～

Nathan called a couple of times each day from the detox center. He was very sick, as anyone who has watched a heroin and cocaine addict detoxing knows. It is heartwrenching to watch them writhing in pain from severe abdominal cramping, accompanied by uncontrollable vomiting and diarrhea. Muscles and bones ache, legs jerk involuntarily, and the person goes through cold sweats, severe depression, and an intense craving for heroin. The meds the nurses at the detox give take the edge off, but it is a walk you must do on your own.

On day five, Nathan called. He was very agitated and wanted to leave, saying the walls were closing in and he had to get out of there.

We talked for forty-five minutes. I told him he had to stay, there was nowhere to go. He had been on the mean streets before, many times, and knew what awaited him there. He eventually calmed down and agreed he would stay.

However, that calm did not last long, and he walked out of the detox, right onto the very streets that he hated and that terrified me.

I had no choice—now I had to turn Nathan in for the bank robbery. It might be the only way to save his life and prevent him from hurting someone else, if he tried that again. He was desperate, so I knew he would.

Nathan is genuinely a gentle, kind person who would never intentionally hurt someone else. I have always believed that. But addiction changes a person. We all have to accept that an addict is dangerous to himself, to you and his family, to his friends and neighbors, and to all of society, at home and in the workplace and on the highways. No one is safe from a hardcore addict. The only way to support a drug habit is stealing and manipulation, lies and violence.

He had to become accountable for his crimes.

～

I called the RCMP detachment and asked to speak to the officer indicated in the newspaper article, but she was off for the next three days. So I asked whether, if I wrote up a letter about a bank robbery, I could leave it in her mailbox. "Absolutely," said the attending officer.

I then sat down and wrote the letter I knew would send my son to prison.

Before you are that desperate to save the life of your adult child, your last option seems almost unthinkable. If you had ever told me I would one day have to turn in my child, I would have said, "Absolutely no way. That would never happen. Bad people go to prison, and my son isn't bad." Now I had to accept that addiction had in fact turned my son into a criminal. You cannot be an addict and not be a criminal as well. The cost of addiction—financial and otherwise—is monumental.

I finished the letter, took it to the RCMP detachment office, and cried all the way home. I was devastated and, once again, both physically and mentally exhausted. It felt like my world had completely fallen apart.

~ 26 ~

"FUCK YOU"

"Don't limit yourself. Many people limit themselves
to what they think they can do. You can go as far as your mind lets you.
What you believe, you can achieve."

~ MARY KAY ASH ~

*I*T WAS NOW 7:00 P.M. I HAD JUST RETURNED FROM THE DETACH-
ment and the phone was ringing. I initially thought it was someone
who had called the wrong number.

"Where the fuck is the $180 you were supposed to fucking send through
Western Union?" It was Nathan but it didn't sound like my son. I thought
maybe he had dialed my number instead of someone else's.

"Nathan, do you know who you are talking to?"

"Yes. Where is the fucking money? You were supposed to send it. It's
not fucking here."

"Nathan, I don't know what you're talking about. What's going on?
Where are you?"

"I'm at a hotel. I don't know the fuck where." I heard several other voices
in the background. He was clearly afraid; I could hear it in his voice.

"These guys are going to fucking kill me tonight if you don't get that fucking $180 here right now. Go and send it now. They are not fucking around. I'll be a fucking dead man."

"Nathan, tell me what hotel you're in. I'll call the police."

"I told you, I don't fucking know. Just get that money wired to me right now or you will be fucking reading about me on the front page of the fucking newspaper tomorrow morning."

The easiest thing for me to do would have been to wire the money. The mom in me wanted to. The co-dependent personality wanted to save him from these guys. I love my son more than I love myself. I would lay down my life in a heartbeat if it meant saving him. But I could no longer "put a Band-Aid on a gunshot wound." That may help for a couple of minutes but it doesn't change or fix the real issue.

Nathan was terrified. I knew he had walked into a situation he was not able to talk or bargain his way out of. In the past when he had been against the wall like this, knowing it was a life or death situation, when he was calling with a pistol shoved in his mouth, I had gotten him the money; there had been no way I was going to lose my son if all I had to do was come up with the money. I knew that this time there was a very real possibility I was going to lose him, if not tonight to these dealers then tomorrow or the next day to a heroin or cocaine overdose. There was something in his voice. He was dying and I was not going to be able to prevent it. All the love in the world could not stop it. Every fiber of my being said this was the end, one way or another. If I rescued him, it was just going to postpone the inevitable. If I didn't, he would be violently abused and left to die. But if he survived, maybe, just maybe, it would be that bottom I had prayed he would hit.

"I'm sorry, Nathan, not anymore. I will do anything in the world to help you get well but I will never again help to keep you sick. I love you so much, Nathan."

"Yeah? Well fuck you." And the phone went dead.

~

The phone number was blocked. I called the RCMP, who told me to call the Vancouver Police Department, since I believed Nathan was still in Vancouver. I explained the situation over the phone to a Vancouver Police District 3 officer, and he put me through to a detective. I again explained the conversation I'd had with Nathan, and the detective was genuinely empathetic. I gave him all of Nathan's information, including an alias he might be using. The detective pulled up Nathan's photo from his police file and said he would get it out to all officers immediately. If any of them saw Nathan, he would call me back.

I waited by the phone.

At 3:00 in the morning, the detective called. He said they had not found Nathan as of yet but that every car had a photo of him. If anyone saw him they would pick him up.

6:30 a.m. The detective called again. The back alleys and dumpsters had been checked, and he had called all the hospitals and checked the morgue. There was no sign of Nathan anywhere. He explained that this was good. He would keep me posted if there were any developments.

I didn't hear anything that day or the next. No call from Nathan. No call from the Vancouver PD or the RCMP.

Then a call came from the detective in Vancouver. An officer had made contact with Nathan. His words haunted me. "He is alive but he's in a bad way." The officer had offered to take him to a shelter, but he had said no.

The officers who walk the beat on the mean streets of Vancouver see it all—all the human suffering, all the despair. They know the people on the streets, see them every day. And they said my son was "in a bad way."

I sensed he was nearing death. "Please, my son, reach out for help. Surely you have realized there is no further bottom to hit. That's it. There is no more."

Because the officer I had sent the note to regarding the bank robbery had not yet arranged a warrant for Nathan's arrest, the officer let him go on his way; he had nothing to hold him on. As an adult, Nathan had a right to walk away.

~

Twenty-four hours later, an officer in Surrey, a suburb of Vancouver, recognized Nathan from the photo sent out about the bank robbery and followed him into a donut shop.

Nathan was hungry and asked for a donut cruller and a cup of tea. Just before that, he had been fronted enough heroin to kill himself. That was his plan. He saw no way out and he was sick and he was tired—resigned that, try as he could, he would never get this monkey off his back. So he would eat the donut cruller and drink his cup of tea, and then he would inject himself and go off to sleep and hopefully death would take him to a better place. After all, he had already been living in hell.

As he turned to leave, he saw the officer watching him. He then noticed a number of police cars parked in front of the donut shop near the door. He knew they were there for him. This was it. Several other officers entered the donut shop. Nathan walked up to the one watching, put his hands out, and said, "I guess you're here for me." The cuffs were put on tightly, but Nathan was used to that.

The officer could see a broken man in front of him. Clearly, Nathan was no threat to their safety, so he loosened the cuffs, which Nathan appreciated. He then led Nathan to his car.

I got a call from the RCMP to say that Nathan was alive and in jail. The following day, a detective from the Serious Crimes Division arrived at my door. Would I consider looking at some photos to see whether I could identify my son in any of them? There were several pictures, some from different angles, some from different bank robberies. As tears burned down my cheeks, I could identify all but one positively; I couldn't be a hundred percent sure whether that last one was Nathan. The detective asked me to sign and date the back of each photo in which I could identify Nathan. He had recorded all of our conversation.

I needed him to know that Nathan was more than a drug addict who had robbed these banks. I asked him whether he had children. He said no but that he and his wife were trying. I told him how much Nathan was loved, that Nathan may have committed criminal acts but that he was my son, and I loved him just as much as the detective's mom loved him. I asked him to remember that every addict he came across in his work was someone's son or daughter, sister or brother, mother or father.

They are more than their addiction. Someone, somewhere, waits for a call from them.

I know. I've waited.

I LOVED SEEING MY SON,
BUT I HATED BEING AT THE PRISON

*"Dreams are renewable. No matter what our age or condition, there are
still untapped possibilities within us and new beauty waiting to be born."*

~ DR. DALE TURNER ~

ETOXING IN A JAIL CELL IS VERY DIFFICULT, AS ANYONE WHO
knows about detoxing can confirm. No medication to help with
some of the anxiety, only one blanket to keep you warm when every shred
of your being is shaking with the chills. You vomit in a pail and double
over with the pain of your body not having its fix. You hurt so bad you
wish you were dead.

"Here, buddy," said a guard as he threw an extra blanket in Nathan's cell.
Nathan was grateful. Really grateful. "Thank you very much."

~

Most inmates in the prison system, possibly as high as 90%, are inside for
crimes in some way related to drug and/or alcohol abuse. The prison system
is full of people battling addiction. These are men and women suffering from

an unforgiving disease spread by dealers and traffickers who get richer as their victims get sicker. They will take you to your knees, take you to your death, and then find another lost soul to continue the cycle.

My son was in prison, but at least he was still alive.

It generally takes him about ten days to detox. I didn't go to see Nathan for two weeks. Then I called the jail to make a visiting appointment. Nathan had put me on his list of approved visitors.

The guard led six of us into the visiting area. Glass separated the inmates from the visitors, and each visitor sat in a separate cubicle. I saw Nathan coming through the door. My heart melted with love and sadness. But I am not a fool and neither is Nathan. He knew I was the one who had turned him in, and I would confirm that with him.

An inmate rarely thinks, "I'm in here because I robbed a bank or committed a murder or any other type of crime." The typical mindset is, "You turned me in. You fucked me over." You become the bad guy because you turned them in. Never mind that they had done the crime. I knew Nathan had mixed emotions about me—love, but also hate. He saw the face of someone he knew loved him unconditionally, while not forgetting that this same person had put him there.

Nathan sat in the pre-trial jail for two and a half months before his case was heard and he was sentenced. It was just me sitting in the courtroom. Nathan was brought in, handcuffed and behind a glass partition. He had been clean and sober now for ten weeks and it showed—he had put some weight on and looked healthy.

He had had two and a half months to sit and think about all that had gone on, and he felt genuine remorse. When I saw him standing there, listening to the proceedings, my eyes filled with tears. I could see his did as well.

The judge read the list of crimes and Nathan pled guilty. Both his court-appointed lawyer and the Crown made recommendations to the judge, who then called me forward. He had read my letter to the RCMP. In an unusual move, he asked me what I would like to have happen.

I had done a lot of research on what was available in both the provincial and the federal prison systems. The provincial prisons were basically hold-ing tanks, offering no real programs to help the prisoners. It was just a lot of waiting and biding time. The sentences were shorter, though, nothing longer than two years less a day.

The federal penitentiary would mean a longer sentence but they offered programs: drug and alcohol counseling, drug maintenance groups, anger management. The prisoners also had the opportunity to work in the prison for a few dollars a day, which helped to pass the time.

Speaking to the judge, I outlined all the programs Nathan had been in over the last sixteen years. I explained that Nathan had a habit of leaving every recovery program he was in. If there was a long-term, locked down program that he could not leave when the going got tough, that would be my first choice. However, I knew that was an unlikely option. My second choice would be for Nathan to be sent to a federal institution, because of the programs available. I explained that I didn't want Nathan to come out of a provincial jail with nothing under his belt but frustration and anger, and having gained no tools in the fight against addiction, so the federal prison system was where Nathan stood the best chance.

The judge agreed and Nathan was sentenced to the federal penitentiary, where the minimum sentence is two years, which is what he received. He would also be on probation for three years after he had served his time, and was given a ten-year ban on the possession of anything that could be used as a weapon.

Nathan looked at me with hate and disgust in his eyes. He had been hoping I was going to in some way try to get him out of this mess, or at least attempt to convince the judge to give a lesser sentence. I understood. I told myself it wasn't *me* he hated, it was the situation he had created. He just didn't know that yet.

So began his two-year sentence. He was put in several federal institu-tions in the BC Lower Mainland, then requested a transfer to Williamhead Penitentiary on Vancouver Island, because they offered a drug program he wanted to take.

He waited for approval of the transfer, not really sure whether he stood a chance of getting it. But after a few weeks, his approval came through. "Pack your bag. You leave here in half an hour for Williamhead." He threw his possessions in a bag and had just enough time to call me with the news.

~

Every institution is different, with its own issues and dangers. You never know what will await you, but you learn. You have to—and quickly.

Williamhead, like many prisons, holds inmates convicted of a wide variety of offences, including murderers, rapists, child molesters, kidnappers, arms dealers, and bank robbers. Many are lifers. Some men went in basically as kids, eighteen or twenty years old, and are now middle-aged or older men with no concept of the world outside, with its cell phones, iPods, ATM machines, and computers, no sense of how people function beyond the prison. Integrating back into mainstream society would be extremely difficult if not nearly impossible for some of them. Thus, the revolving door of release, followed by reoffending and reincarceration. They have no idea of how life works on the outside anymore.

A corrections officer's responsibility is to protect society by insuring inmates do not escape, to at all times monitor the situation within the prison, and to try and maintain law and order there. In most situations, though, a corrections officer will not see an altercation between inmates. Prison violence is a harsh reality, and this isn't helped by overcrowding. Too many inmates often leads to double bunking, which in turn raises the stress and violence levels. Gangs are also a fact of life inside, and they are always looking for recruits as new prisoners enter the system.

Prisoners often possess a combination of creativity, inventiveness, and talent: ketchup packets or fruit, along with some bread, make prison brew; a Walkman can be converted into an instrument used to tattoo. Unfortunately, their creativity is overshadowed by violence and manipulation.

Everyday items become tools of violence. Butter or margarine packets are heated to boiling in a microwave, mixed with sugar or syrup for stickiness, then thrown in an inmate's face: this is "getting hot buttered." A simple toothbrush filed to a point makes a convenient shank, as do any number of other things.

Each time Nathan was released after being incarcerated, his level of anxiety was very high for several days. In the system, you have to keep this invisible bubble around you and not let anyone penetrate it, otherwise you jeopardize your safety and security. Inside prison, if someone enters this invisible bubble—gets too close—a threatening situation could result, so the inmate's guard is always up. There is always an awareness of potential danger.

Once an inmate is released, it is difficult to shed that bubble. Just walking down a street where everyone brushes against each other increases that high level of anxiety. They are inside your bubble—so watch your back.

~

It was at this time that I hit my all-time low. Although I was working and doing everything that "needed" to be done, inside I was falling apart, but I didn't realize it.

I became so obsessed with "finding a safe place" where Nathan could go once his incarceration ended—away from easy access to drugs, away from the violence of gangs and away from traffickers—that it became all consuming.

I came up with an idea. As insane as it was and as insane as it will sound to anyone else, I know as a parent struggling with your child's addiction as well, you will understand my desperation.

I searched and searched on the Internet for isolated acreages and I eventually found one. It was in the Chilcotin, a beautiful, pristine and very isolated mountainous area of British Columbia. So isolated, in fact, that electricity didn't extend to that area. It was set up to be a very rustic wilderness trail-riding adventure facility. The owners were eager to sell the property and it was priced accordingly.

I made an offer and it was accepted. I convinced myself and everyone else that this was "my dream." In my mind, it would be like the television show some years back with Michael Landon, "Little House on the Prairie," where goodness always prevailed. Nathan could "start over—start fresh" when he was released from prison. Now the insanity of this all was that Nathan had never given even the slightest indication of any interest in that type of lifestyle. But oh, the lengths we parents will go to, to try and help our addicted loved ones! As if we have any control!

My youngest daughter, Jazz, loved animals and by that time had been working on ranches in Alberta. Her dream was to one day own acreage where she could raise horses. Her boyfriend's passion was the same as hers. Jazz had bravely battled a serious illness herself for a couple of years and since her passion was horses, to me this seemed like a win/win situation.

The previous eighteen months had taken a huge toll on me and all of us. Losing my Dad, who was my dear, dear friend, from the fire. My precious grandson's death from a car accident and seeing the devastation of that loss for my daughter Jada, who was a loving, caring mom. Feeling absolute heartbreak for my beautiful granddaughter working through the loss of her brother, whom she adored. Knowing I could not stop my daughter's horrific pain. All I could do was be there when she cried and there when she needed someone to be angry at. There is no greater pain than for a mother to lose her child.

Nathan's dramatic escalation in his drug use. The very real awareness that he could die at any time. The frightening drive to Vancouver on New Year's Eve when he was at risk of losing his arms and in an angry psychosis. The trips to the USA for treatment, and all the drama surrounding that. The bank robberies that I turned him in for and my testimony at his hearing that sealed his fate and sent him to prison. I was heartbroken.

The collateral damage of addiction is extensive. It had brought me to my knees. My world was crashing down on me.

To finalize the sale agreement, I drove five hours north, met up with the realtor handling the sale of the isolated acreage, and drove another three hours with her to get there. For every mile I got closer to the ranch, I knew in my heart I was one mile further away from where I needed to be. It was minus 30 degrees Celsius, and ice and snow covered everything. A foal had been killed by a cougar and there was blood in the snow. It was devastating to me.

What had I done? I started crying and try as I did, I could not stop. I drove eight hours home. I didn't want to sell my house. I didn't want to live in isolation where cougars, wolves and grizzly bears roamed. Where there was no electricity. Where I would be away from my family. Away from everything I knew. Where I would basically be snowed in for seven months of the year. What had I been thinking? In my desperation to "save" my son from addiction I had completely "lost" myself.

I needed to shut down. I was unable to stop crying and I cried for the next three days.

How could I get out of the mess I had gotten myself into? What had I been thinking? With the help of my daughter Kiara, a friend, a lawyer and my doctor of twenty years, I was eventually able to negotiate a financial settlement that allowed me to retract my offer to purchase the wilderness acreage and to reverse the offer I had accepted for the purchase of my home.

I had always prided myself in my ability to handle whatever came my way. But, just as a strong giant oak tree will eventually fall if it is hit too many times with an axe—I had had too many emotional blows and I fell also.

Within a week, I picked myself up and was back working and doing what needed to be done. But for perhaps the first time I had to admit to myself that I too was fragile.

~

I visited Nathan every weekend when he was in an institution on the Lower Mainland and every second weekend when he was on the island. The visits meant a lot to both of us.

When he was in Williamhead, I would get up at 4:00 a.m., shower and dress, and reach the ferry terminal by 5:30 so I could get in the lineup and be assured of a place. The ferry took an hour and a half, then it was three quarters of an hour's drive to the prison.

Show ID, sign in, put all belongings in lockers, get tested for drugs, and go through security. Visitors could take $20 in change to use at the canteen. That's a prisoner's high point, having a visitor and something from the canteen. Nathan liked to order springs rolls and Earl Grey tea. I generally just had a pop, saving the money for Nathan to use. Whatever you didn't spend you had to take home—no leaving the inmate money or anything purchased at the canteen, not even a package of gum. I'd stay for the entire allotted visiting time, and we'd play cards or board games, or walk and talk.

Leaving was always difficult, but not nearly as difficult as when I'd had to walk away from Nathan on the street.

~

I think that for the first time in his life, Nathan found himself. Prison may be an unlikely place to find yourself, but others before him have as well. Only the acceptance of hitting bottom allows you to look up. That is the only way to go if you want to survive.

Eventually, his anger towards me for turning him in passed, but I think he still blamed me instead of himself for being incarcerated, although he slowly started taking responsibility for that.

He was liked well enough amongst his prison inmates. I never saw any indication that he had been in an altercation, as I had when he was first arrested: two inmates jumped him in his cell for no apparent reason other than to lay a beating. At that time I asked Nathan about the cuts and bruises on his face, but he said he'd just fallen. I knew different and was devastated. Nathan also knew that I knew, but in his own way he thought he was protecting me.

Over time, I found peace while Nathan was in prison. What a thing for a mother to say. But it was true. As much as I worried about Nathan's safety inside the system, I had worried much, much more when he was outside, using and on the streets. The only time I seemed to get a half-decent night's sleep was when Nathan was either in a treatment facility or incarcerated.

~ 28 ~

LETTERS TO THE PAROLE BOARD

*"Lots of people want to ride with you in the limo,
but what you want is someone who will take the bus with you
when the limo breaks down."*

~ OPRAH WINFREY ~

*"A true friend is someone who reaches for your hand
and touches your heart."*

~ AUTHOR UNKNOWN ~

07/02/2008 18:41 FAX ⌷001

```
********************
***   TX REPORT   ***
********************

TRANSMISSION OK

TX/RX NO            1529
CONNECTION TEL               16048702498
SUBADDRESS
CONNECTION ID
ST. TIME           07/02 18:40
USAGE T            01'02
PGS. SENT          7
RESULT             OK
```

To:

National Parole Board
Suite 305 - 32315 South Fraser Way
Abbottsford, B.C. V2T 1W6

RE: ▮▮▮▮▮▮▮▮▮▮▮▮

   FPS ▮▮▮▮▮▮

LETTERS: - ▮▮▮▮▮▮▮▮▮▮
         - ▮▮▮▮▮▮▮▮▮▮
         - ▮▮▮▮▮▮▮▮▮▮
         - ▮▮▮▮▮▮▮▮▮▮
         - ▮▮▮▮▮▮▮▮▮▮

Re:

FPS

July 2, 2008

To whom it may concern,

We have known ██████████ for 8 years. We are very good friends with his mother June. We have had many fun evenings playing cards with ████ We have always known ████ when he is clean to be very kind and helping, always asking if there is anything he can do to help us. We were in a car accident last year and ████ came into the hospital to see me after my surgery and kindly stayed and helped ████ clean up after I had been very ill, I certainly do not know many young men that would even take the time to come and see me let alone help clean up, we were very impressed by his kindness.

I know that ████ family has always been very supportive of ████ and always will be. As good family friends we also will be very supportive of him to live a clean and productive life in the future.

Sincerely,

Home phone #

E-mail:

Re:

FPS ▓▓▓▓▓▓▓

June 27, 2008

RE: ▓▓▓▓▓▓▓▓ for Corrections Canada.

Dear Sir/Madame,

I have known ▓▓▓ for approximately 8 years. My ▓▓▓▓ attended ▓▓▓▓ Mothers ▓▓▓▓▓▓▓ 7 years. During this time I have had numerous interactions with ▓▓▓. He has always been very friendly and polite to my children and myself. I hired ▓▓▓ one spring to do some yard work around my home. It was a very large task and he worked very diligently over the course of a week. He did a great job and I would recommend him to others. ▓▓▓ Mother June is a wonderful Woman that creates a great environment for the ▓▓▓ attending her ▓▓▓ and for her family. She is a wonderful person and Mother. With June and other family members and friends, ▓▓▓ will have lots of love and support in his transition back into society.

Kindest Regards,

E-mail: ▓▓▓▓▓▓▓▓▓▓

Cell: ▓▓▓▓▓▓▓

July 1st, 2008

Re:

FPS

Corrections Canada
Re:

To whom it may concern;

    I am writing this letter in support of ▮ I am fully aware of all the troubles he has endured and would gladly stand by him and his family in this time of rebuilding. I believe that is so important for him to know that he has a strong support group in place. I had met ▮ 11 years ago through his Sister and my best friend, ▮ I can honestly say that he is a kind, generous and funny guy who was always a polite gentleman whenever he was around me or my children. This is definitely not a person to give up on. I have always been able to see ▮ for who he is and not for what his addiction enabled him to become.

    ▮ is truly a good guy whom I would be willing to help out in any situation in any time of need.

Sincerely,

Re: ███████████████████

F PS ███████████

June 28, 2008

Attention: **Corrections Canada**
To Whom It May Concern:

Please accept this letter as a character reference for ████████ I have personally known ████ for eight plus years. I met ████ when I enrolled ████████████ into his mother's ████████ Since that time, ████ family has become an extended part of my family.

I have always found ████ to be a genuinely kind, considerate and polite young man. I have even had the opportunity to see ████ dress up as Santa Claus for the ████████████ Christmas Party. ████ has done some work at my home in the past landscaping and basically getting my garden beds in order after being grown over in weeds for two year. I found ████ to be an extremely conscientious and thorough worker, never once cutting corners. I recall having ████ into the house for a meal in appreciation of his hard work and having a delightful conversation. Again he was extremely polite and kind.

I think my most touching memory of ████ was when he delivered the Eulogy at his Grandfathers funeral. Delivering a message on such an emotional day can be a daunting task for anyone; however, he delivered a heartwarming and touching tribute to "Pops."

████ has an extremely loving and supportive family who are there to provide support. He also has several friends, like myself, who are committed to helping him transition back to the life he so truly deserves. I have applied for and been granted Visitors privileges with ████ because I am committed to helping him however I can, even if that just means visiting. I will also be available to visit with ████ once he returns home.

As a Human Resources professional with 15 years experience in my field I have the privilege of working with people at all levels and all professions. As a result, I feel confident in my abilities to understand people. I believe in ████ and his commitment to overcome the serious challenges he has undergone in the past.

Although I have been provided with the opportunity to express my support and belief in ████ I think his actions and commitment to change and growth over the past several months speak for themselves.

If I can provide any more information on behalf of ████, please do not hesitate to contact me directly at ████████

Kind Regards,

████████████

Re: ▓▓▓▓▓▓▓▓▓▓▓▓▓ — F PS ▓▓▓▓▓▓▓▓

July 1, 2008

To Whom it may concern,

I am writing on behalf of my brother ▓▓▓▓▓▓. Drug use has always been ▓▓▓ problem, and even though I may not have supported the choices he made as a drug-user, there has never been a time when I didn't support ▓▓▓ as a person. My brother is one of the nicest people I've ever met. He is respectful, hardworking, and genuinely caring. Even at his worst, it was impossible to give up on ▓▓▓ because you could see the potential in him, the possibility.

I recently visited with ▓▓▓ at William Head Institution, and was amazed by the change in him. He didn't have one excuse for anything that has happened to him, and credits this time with saving his life. For the first time in as long as I can remember, he is thinking clearly, and with real hope for the future. He talked about how much time he has wasted, and how lucky he feels to have the chance to turn things around. I look forward to helping him do this.

▓▓▓ has a very strong support system surrounding him -- family and friends - all of us who love him, and are willing to help him in any way we can to make the transition to a drug-free life.

Sincerely,

Re: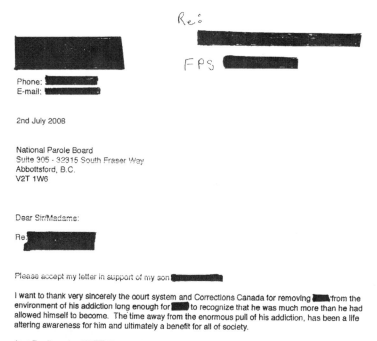

FPS ▮▮▮▮▮▮▮▮

Phone: ▮▮▮▮▮▮
E-mail: ▮▮▮▮▮▮▮

2nd July 2008

National Parole Board
Suite 305 - 32315 South Fraser Way
Abbottsford, B.C.
V2T 1W6

Dear Sir/Madame:

Re: ▮▮▮▮▮▮▮▮

Please accept my letter in support of my son ▮▮▮▮▮▮▮▮

I want to thank very sincerely the court system and Corrections Canada for removing ▮▮▮ from the environment of his addiction long enough for ▮▮▮ to recognize that he was much more than he had allowed himself to become. The time away from the enormous pull of his addiction, has been a life altering awareness for him and ultimately a benefit for all of society.

As a Family and as ▮▮▮ Mom, we have never given up on ▮▮▮ because we saw ▮▮▮ for who he was - he was always much more than his addiction. He is an extremely kind, considerate and gentle person. He is polite, thoughtful, respectful and hardworking. ▮▮▮ has no mean-ness in him. In all of his life - I have never heard him say an unkind word about anyone.

▮▮▮ has expressed to me on several occassions, now badly he feels for the fear and anxiety he very obviously caused the tellers he approached. He has true remorse. He has come to terms with just how far his addiction had taken him and he is very sorry.

▮▮▮ has also told me that this time in incarceration has saved his life.

Each visit I have with ▮▮▮ is more and more enjoyable. He has become the man he was meant to be. The one I always knew was there.

▮▮▮ has a very strong Family support system. His sister's, brother and I, as well as Family Friends will do everything possible to help and encourage ▮▮▮ to re-integrate back into main stream society. We will encourage and support ▮▮▮ completely to live a drug-free life. We will also support ▮▮▮ in decisions he makes as to courses he wants to take that will allow him to become the productive and contributing member of society he truly wants to be.

▮▮▮ has said to me - "Prison is not a revolving door for me Mom - I will never be back" and "I finally have my life back - this saved my life" and "I was always looking for an easy way - but there is only one way Mom - the right way".

██████ and our Family have true gratitude.

Should you make the decision to release ██████ he will not let you down. He will not let himself down. The balance of ██████ life will be much different - he has the knowledge of where addiction can take you and the wisdom and committment to know he won't go back.

Always in the past I had deep hope for a turn-around but no clear expectation. Today I have that expectation.

Very Sincerely,

████████████████████

██████████████

Re: ████████████████████████

FPS ████████████████

Government
of Canada

Gouvernement
du Canada

National Parole Board
Pacific Regional Office
305-32315 South Fraser Way
Abbotsford, B.C. V2T 1W6

Commission nationale des
libérations conditionnelles
Région du Pacifique
Abbotsford, (C.B.) V2T 1W6

Tel: (604) 870-2468
Fax: (604) 870-2498

2008 July 08

Dear ███████████

I am writing in response to your letter of support, in relation to ████████████████ which was received in our office on July 4, 2008.

Your letter has been placed on the National Parole Board file and will be available for Board Members to review prior to any future conditional release decisions that ███ ████████ may have. ████████████ and to Correctional Services of Canada staff also have copies of this letter.

Thank you.

███████████
Case Review Officer

Canadä

~ 29 ~

ON PAROLE AND ON THE LAM

"The secret of health for both mind and body is not to mourn for the past,
worry about the future, or anticipate troubles but to live in the
present moment wisely and earnestly."

~ BUDDHA ~

WHEN NATHAN WAS FIRST RELEASED ON PAROLE, HE WENT TO a halfway house on Vancouver Island. He made friends at NA and AA meetings and felt really comfortable there. He even mentioned that when he finished his parole, he would probably stay on the island. Then he learned he was being transferred to a halfway house on the mainland. Shortly after that transfer, Nathan was sent back to prison for "deteriorating attitude." That threw him and surprised me. I had thought he was doing well.

Two days after him being reincarcerated, I had a call from a detective at the RCMP Serious Crimes Division, asking whether I could come in to see her when I got off work. She didn't indicate what she wanted to talk to me about, and I was naturally quite concerned. When I arrived at the detachment office, the detective was very nice and I immediately liked her. She asked me to look at some still photos and video surveillance.

A bank had been robbed near the halfway house where Nathan had been housed. The robber fit Nathan's description—down to the hairstyle and facial hair. Could I please look through all the data and either confirm or dismiss Nathan as a suspect? She indicated she knew I would tell her the truth, as one of her coworkers was the detective who had brought the photos of the initial bank robberies, in which I had identified the robber as my son.

Yes, I would absolutely tell her the truth one way or the other, but I prayed it would not be Nathan in the pictures.

I looked at all the photos and went frame by frame through the surveillance tape. This man certainly had a resemblance to Nathan, but thankfully, I could absolutely be sure, 100% sure, it was not him. The detective thanked me, saying they would eliminate Nathan as a suspect and go in a different direction.

Two days later, Nathan was released from prison again. I had to assume that the "deteriorating attitude" was perhaps in some way connected to the bank robbery, though of course I am not sure.

~

Upon his release, he was sent to another halfway house, this one in North Vancouver. He liked it well enough there, much more so than the previous one, though he said one staff member was "a dick."

Over time, I came to believe that Nathan was perhaps right. The guy was certainly nice to me when I stopped by, but I noticed he had a way of putting down the parolees. Not cool. Not necessary. We have to remember that every person is struggling in a difficult world. Parolees already have negative self-images, and each is struggling in his own way. Why put them down and make them feel embarrassed in front of someone they don't even know?

His behaviour was completely unnecessary and just plain mean.

Nathan worked on the required programs, but all he really wanted was to go home. That's a privilege, though, not a right, once you cross that line into the prison system, and it was one he would not be granted for quite some time.

~

Nathan contacted an old boss in the construction business who would hire him back. His parole officer gave him permission to work at a bridge site; he could leave the halfway house at 5:00 a.m. and had to be back by 5:00 p.m. Everything was going well. He was happy to be working and away from the halfway house for twelve hours each day.

Friday afternoon, I got a call from Nathan. He said his boss had been called out of town and left him supervisor for the day. It had rained quite heavily the previous few days, and the site was very muddy. As a result, a piece of heavy equipment had gotten stuck in the mud. They had tried and tried to get it out, to no avail. Since the forecast was for a dry weekend, Nathan had sent the guys home for the rest of the day rather than risk getting another piece of equipment stuck in the muddy trenches.

The guys got their paychecks and called it a day.

If what follows hadn't landed him back in the prison system and caused me so much worry, you would almost think it was a pilot episode for a new sitcom. But it was no sitcom; it was our lives.

~

Nathan didn't call again Friday or Saturday, as he usually did. Saturday evening, I tried calling the halfway house and left a message on voicemail. Normally he would call back. When I didn't hear anything by Sunday afternoon, I took a drive to North Vancouver.

Nathan was not there. They said he hadn't returned to the halfway house on Friday. "He's obviously out using. He got his paycheck. We see this all the time. Since he didn't come back, there is a warrant out for his arrest," explained the supervisor. He was very kind, a genuinely caring man, and said he was sorry he did not have better news.

~

I went into the "mom mode." Maybe I was in denial. No—I was definitely in denial. I just couldn't believe it. I wouldn't believe it. He had been clean and sober a year and a half now. No way did I want to believe he had gone out using. He had been so proud of himself and really doing well.

So this was my denial: "Maybe he stayed after the guys left work on Friday. Perhaps he tried on his own to get the stuck tractor out of the mud at the construction site. What if, when he was trying to do that, something rolled on his leg and he couldn't get out, he was trapped? Everyone left and no one knew. Time for Mom to go to the rescue."

We do this and have been doing this for years. This is the insanity of the disease of addiction. We know, but somehow we just can't believe it could happen again. Not after all this time.

Now, if I'd had no mom mode, I would have accepted that yes, he had gone out and gotten drunk or high and we'd have to wait until he either got caught or turned himself in. I would have gone home, made a cup of tea, and just had one of those "damn you, Nathan" moments, accepting the situation for what it was.

But no. I was in mom mode and driving miles and miles to a construction site, not having a clue of exactly where I was going. In fact, I didn't even know what side of the bridge he was working on. But I had to find my son. I was even praying that he was stuck under a piece of equipment. That would have been better than having him using.

Finally, I was at the construction site. It was massive and surrounded by an eight-foot fence. So there I was, this crazy, fifty-five-year-old, white-haired lady trying to scale a fence because I wanted to believe my son was there. My jeans got caught on a nail and I couldn't unsnag them. The nail was keeping me from either getting up and over the fence or getting down from it. I'm sure this would have made it on America's Funniest Home Videos.

Anyways, I finally got loose from the nail and over the fence I climbed. I searched everywhere but did not see Nathan or his car.

This is the insanity of addiction. Was my behavior not completely insane? Yes it was and I have to own that!!

~

He was not there. I drove home quietly, letting the wind blow in my face; I needed the wind to keep me from crying.

When I got home, I checked for messages. There was one from the halfway house. All I could think while dialing the phone was, "Thank you God," expecting them to say he was back.

No. Nathan apparently had gotten drunk Friday night. He didn't want to go back to the halfway house because drinking violated one of the conditions of his parole and he didn't want to be sent back to jail for the violation.

So what would you do if you drank and missed your curfew and risked being sent back to prison? Of course, you would go on the run—not!!! But yes, that is exactly what they did, "they" being Nathan and his new girlfriend, Ali.

After a night of drinking, Nathan and Ali went to the First Nations reserve where her sister, brother-in-law, and two children lived. Her brother-in-law was First Nations, and their thinking was that the police would not go on reserve land; they had no jurisdiction to check on parole violations there.

By the next morning, all Nathan could think about was, "What the hell did I do now?"

Ali's brother-in-law had bonded with Nathan and suggested he should stay on the reserve with them; they could all "fish and make a living there."

Meanwhile, I was just praying Nathan would call the police station and let them know he was coming to turn himself in. But that never happened because when he drove the brother-in-law to a crack house, the police who were watching the house arrested Nathan while he was waiting in the car.

So whereas he would have had a drinking violation if he had gone back to the halfway house, that fight-or-flight adrenalin rush, that addict's "stinking thinking" kicked in and he ran. Now he had a whole list of violations: drinking, missing curfew, not returning to the halfway house, going on the run, socializing with a known drug addict, and on and on. Of course, Nathan's mind was then clear and he was ashamed and disappointed in himself, worried about the fall-out and how everyone would react.

All I could feel was gratitude that he was back in the prison system and not stoned or dead somewhere. Only the mom of an addict is grateful when her child is incarcerated. At least, for that time, he is not doing what an addict does.

∽

When Nathan was arrested, his car was impounded about 300 km, or approximately 200 miles, away. Nathan told the police that the car could be released to his girlfriend.

Ali called me the next day. She didn't have the money to get the car out of impound; could we come and do that? Michael again stepped up to the plate. I handed him my credit card to pay the impound fee but he said, "No, Mom, I'll take care of it."

I called Ali to let her know Michael was about to leave and asked her whether she was okay to drive Nathan's car back. She did not know how to drive a standard, but said that if Michael could drive Nathan's car she could drive Michael's. Okay, that would work. Then she said, "I've never had a driver's license, but I can drive an automatic really well."

All I could think of was, "Please tell me I didn't hear that logic."

"So what you are telling me is that you cannot drive Michael's vehicle back?"

"Oh sure I can, I just won't get caught."

Right. The prison system is chock full of people who were sure they would never get caught. Just like Nathan! But I recognize Ali was only trying to be helpful. I know she felt bad about the whole situation. But she was not the one responsible for what happened. Nathan had to own the problem. He made the decision to run. No one forced him.

Fortunately, our friend Jeff came to the rescue again. Jeff and Michael drove to meet up with Ali and get the car out of the impound. Jeff would drive Michael's truck back, and Michael would drive Nathan's car home. Should be simple enough. But of course, nothing about this whole situation had been simple.

There was something to do with the paperwork not being in order at the impound, so they had to wait six hours for the arresting officer to come in for his shift before it could be straightened out. All told, Jeff and Michael spent two and a half hours driving there, an hour trying to convince impound to release the car, half an hour going back to the police station, six hours waiting for shift change, half an hour returning to the impound, more time waiting in the lineup to pay, and then two and a half hours driving back home.

When Michael and Jeff arrived, all Michael could say was, "Thirteen fucking hours, thirteen fucking hours, because of two fucking idiots."

Michael's outburst was simply indicative of his frustration. He loved his brother but he was completely exasperated and tired.

The snowball effect of addiction is massive. For many, what seems like a simple decision, to have a drink, for an addict doesn't stop there. That decision causes serious implications that affect not just the person addicted but everyone around who loves the addict and has to once again "clean up the mess."

The reason they made all the effort to get the car back was that I had signed for the financing of that car. If it hadn't been for that, we would have just left it there. Repercussions for bad decisions—another in the long list of mistakes I have made in the name of love. I realized that if he hadn't had that vehicle, he may not have been able to go on the lam, at least not in that manner. So, I transferred the car back into my name. I tried to sell it on Craigslist, but the country was now in a recession and I didn't receive a single call.

～

Nathan was genuinely sorry. He knew he had screwed up and couldn't change that, but he was sorry for all the worry he had caused. Still, he was probably more sorry because he had gotten caught and landed his "sorry ass" back in prison. Again, though, I gave a prayer of thanks that Nathan was being held accountable for his actions. His good looks and great personality no longer got him out of the messes he created.

I accept that with each relapse, Nathan is learning something he needs to grasp before he can lead the life he is meant to live. I have come to accept that when a person—my son, anyone—has for eighteen years been a law-breaker, a criminal living with and associating with criminals and embedded in that mindset, a change may not happen overnight. We want it to. I think they want it as well. But I believe that too often, when the going gets tough, the tough screw up. Plain and simple. That is what they have gotten used to doing. They don't think, they just react.

Unfortunately, that too often is their reality, and so it becomes our reality. We have to accept that changes won't happen in our time frame, but we keep praying that the change will come and that it will be permanent.

~

Nathan went back to prison for this latest escapade. After he had served his time, the halfway house in North Vancouver agreed to take him back. They had several stipulations, though. He could not have access to a vehicle. He could not go back to work; instead, he had to work a program for repeat offenders. He had a 6:00 p.m. nightly curfew. They no longer wanted his girlfriend coming by on a regular basis. She could come only once a week for a designated period. All the previous stipulations also remained in effect.

Nathan and Ali found ways around the stipulations by meeting up at a mall or shop or park each day. Unfortunately, he treated the rules as stumbling blocks instead of stepping stones towards responsible behavior.

And then the day came when Nathan was granted statutory release from the prison system. He remained on parole and saw his parole officer every week, underwent random drug testing, saw a psychologist twice a month, and went to a drug maintenance program weekly. The release stipulations were that he must live with me, hold a full-time job, not drink, not use drugs, possess no weapons, not associate with known criminals, and keep the peace.

To you or I that would seem a more than reasonable set of expectations and quite simple. Just stick to that and there is no trouble. Mess up and you go back to prison.

~

When Nathan is clean and sober he is a hard worker; he can easily do the work of two men and takes pride in his work.

It's not easy for federal inmates on parole to get jobs. They have a lot of baggage and are competing with people who don't. Many are simply unreliable and end up not showing up for a shift. Others really want to change and make a fresh start. A lot of employers understandably shy away from hiring an ex-con or a parolee. Why should they take a risk when a hundred others with a résumé and a letter of recommendation are also applying? This is unfortunate for the ones who really want to bring about a change in their lives, making an uphill battle even steeper. Unless an ex-con or parolee has positive people on the outside, willing to give him another chance, prison life all too often becomes a revolving door. Crime is a familiar fallback.

Not an excuse by any means, but a simple reality.

So once again, Nathan was on the job hunt. He went out knocking on every door he could until he was able to secure employment, again in the construction industry. He was up front with his boss, telling him that on Thursdays he would have to leave early for his parole, psychologist, and drug maintenance appointments. He said that his parole officer could show up at the site for sporadic checks. The man respected his honesty and even opened up about his own troubled past.

~ 30 ~

I ACCEPT THAT WITH EACH STUMBLE, NATHAN IS LEARNING SOMETHING ESSENTIAL

"We would accomplish many more things
if we did not think of them as impossible."

~ CHRETIEN MALESHERBES ~

O N THE OUTSIDE, THINGS APPEARED TO BE GOING WELL. NATHAN was living at home, going to work and the gym, and attending NA and AA meetings around his work schedule. But he wasn't "living the program." He started drinking a bit, then more heavily. He got caught for driving under the influence, was given a 24-hour driving suspension and held overnight in the "drunk tank," and then was free to go. I never quite understood why he wasn't returned to the prison system for breaching a condition of his parole, as this breach would most certainly have shown up when his parole officer pulled up his file. I was glad he had gotten caught. I don't want drunk drivers on the road, putting innocent people at risk. I believe drunk drivers should be given jail time—they wreak havoc every day, destroying lives.

Again, it had become obvious that Nathan needed several wake-up calls to learn the lessons. Progress, not perfection. Sometimes progress slips back. But if our addict starts drinking it is not long before the need for cocaine or other stimulants comes into play.

He stayed out one night, coming home around 5:00 a.m. I heard him pull into the driveway, so I got up and went outside. We know when our loved ones have been using. Oh, they can be very "straight" and convincing after years of practice, but we can tell. We see it in their eyes, their demeanor, their body language. I asked him immediately whether he had been using, and of course he said no. "I'm just not feeling well. I have a migraine, maybe the flu coming on, and I fell asleep on a friend's couch, watching a movie."

He slept all day and through the night.

Of course I knew, and he knew that I knew.

The next morning, he said he had been to a bar, was drinking pretty heavily, and did three lines of cocaine. Then he thought, "What the hell have I done now?" He left the bar, slept in the car, and came home in the morning. He said he was going to tell his parole officer at his next appointment.

Instead of sending him back to prison, his parole officer said she was going to up his drug testing; instead of random testing a couple of times a month, it would be weekly. And instead of talking to the psychologist twice a month, it would be upped to every week. The DUI hadn't shown up on his file yet. He didn't want it to, for more than one reason.

A few days earlier, Nathan had told me that he realized his relationship with Ali wasn't healthy for either of them. They had been fighting a lot, and he said he was going to tell her it was best if they went their separate ways. Negative buttons were being pushed and the relationship had become toxic for both of them. He knew Ali felt the same way he did.

However, the day he went to talk to her, Ali told him she was pregnant.

They were shocked. Doctors had told her that she was left unable to get pregnant from previous years when she struggled with severe anorexia, and bulimia. Nathan told her that if she decided to have an abortion, he would support that decision and go with her; or, if she decided to continue with the pregnancy, he would support that decision and together they would love and treasure their child. They could make it work.

Nathan felt there was nothing he wanted more in the world than to be a dad. Initially, they took the romanticized approach—excited at the prospect of being a family, imagining how perfect life would be. Then reality set in and tough but necessary questions came into play.

The realization of being pregnant naturally caused Ali a lot of anxiety. She was torn and scared, and her fears manifested in different ways. I am certain that, without exception, every unmarried girl faced with an unplanned pregnancy goes through a whole gamut of emotions. She had to consider every possible option available to her. "What will be the best decision for me and for this child? Should I terminate this pregnancy? Should I carry this baby to term and stay as healthy as possible? Should I then give the infant to a loving couple who desperately want a child? Or will I be able to keep my baby and care for it and give it the best life I can? Will the father step up to the plate? How is my support system?" These are absolutely vital questions; a beautiful, innocent new life depends on the woman's decisions.

Their relationship had been toxic prior to Ali becoming pregnant, and neither of them were happy in the relationship. So this made it even more difficult. Emotions changed from joy to resentment at times. In her frustration, she told Nathan that she might have the baby and then move and never tell him where.

I might not have agreed with that approach, but I certainly understood on some level.

~

Life can certainly be an emotional roller coaster—who knows that better than the parent of an addict? And all too often, emotional roller coasters mean addicts go off the rails. But it is their own choice to go back to using. No one can "make you use." Unfortunately, if the addict has not developed the healthy coping skills that are absolutely crucial to sobriety and hasn't completely committed to living his program clean and sober, stress and head games send him right back to drugs and alcohol. Instead of reaching out, he goes back to the habitual brand of solace.

Unfortunately, Nathan made all the wrong choices. His drinking escalated and, in all likelihood, so did his drug use. Addicts when using think only of themselves, and that selfishness meant that Ali would not have Nathan around for support during most of the pregnancy. She basically carried the child alone—and that was not fair.

It was after midnight. We always braced for trouble when the phone rang that late. Michael was still awake and picked up the phone. It was Nathan, hysterical—he had just wrapped the car around a utility pole. Michael brought the phone up to my room and woke me up.

Nathan said, "I was not drinking. I was coming home and I hit water on the road and I lost control of the car and hit a pole, so I ran. I am not going back to jail."

I could hear sirens and emergency vehicles in the background. "Nathan, go back to the accident. Michael and I will be right there."

"No, Mom, I'm not going back. I'm going to wait half an hour and report the car stolen."

"Nathan, no, you go back to the accident. Do the right thing. Tell them what happened. Accidents happen. Don't run, you'll make this worse, and do not file a false police report."

"No. I can't go back."

"Nathan, do the right thing. We'll be right there to support you. Are you hurt?"

"Yes, I really hurt my knees, legs, and hips. My head and neck too."

"Go back to the scene, Nathan. You need medical attention. Don't make a simple situation into a really bad situation for yourself."

The phone went dead. I kept dialing his cell phone but later found out it had been crushed in the accident; he had used a pay phone at a gas station.

I sat by the phone, a sickeningly familiar situation, waiting for the next call. It came from an RCMP officer who had attended the scene. "If you want to know where your car is, it's been put on a flat bed and taken to the impound. Do you know who was driving your car? We believe we know, but we have no proof."

"Yes, it was my son Nathan. He called right after the accident happened. He was scared and ran and would not go back to the scene."

"Was he hurt?" I told him what Nathan had said. "Well, the next time you're talking to him, tell him to go to the hospital and get checked over, and then turn himself in."

Nathan never did go to the hospital or the doctor. Instead, he hid, staying with various buddies here and there the following week. I spoke to his parole officer several times that week. We were both on the same page: get Nathan into custody before he makes this matter any worse.

Eight days later, Nathan showed up and told me he was going to shower and shave, put on clean clothes, and turn himself in. He had already called his parole officer, who would be waiting for him. The last place he wanted to go was back to prison. He knew that this time, he would likely have to finish his sentence inside. Before leaving, he said, "I love you, Mom."

And as I always do, I said, "I love you more."

~ 31 ~

THE REVOLVING DOOR

"Good habits are as easy to form as bad ones."

~ TIM MCCARVER ~

I WOULD NOT SEE NATHAN UNTIL HE GOT RELEASED. I HAD told him when he got out the last time that he'd better plan on never going back, because I would never again visit him in a prison. I hated everything about it. I had visited him regularly in the different jails and prisons far too often because of his own actions. But I was done with that now. So this time, he was going to prison knowing he would not be getting visitors. But he had to realize it was all his own doing.

He was put in one of the harshest prisons on the Lower Mainland. As he always has when incarcerated, Nathan phoned daily. I'd ask him how he was and he always said fine. But nothing about prison is fine, and he hoped for a transfer out of that particular prison.

A few weeks later, Nathan was transferred back to Williamhead on Vancouver Island. He was relieved—he knew how Williamhead worked and was grateful to go back there, where he would still know many of the inmates.

Once again he worked the programs, and once again he was determined to never go back.

~ 32 ~

THE WARMTH IN HIS EYES SEEMED GONE

"Being defeated is often only a temporary condition.
Giving up is what makes it permanent."

~ MARILYN VOS SAVANT ~

$\int$O THERE I WAS, AT THE FERRY TERMINAL. IT WAS CHRISTMAS
Eve and my son was coming home. I was anxious to see him—it had
been a long time. But I noticed a difference: there was an "edge" to him,
and the warmth in his eyes seemed gone. How would this difference play
out? Eventually I would know, but that day we hugged and talked, then got
going. He had just a two-hour window to check in with a new parole officer
and at the police station.

While Nathan had been in prison this latest time, the RCMP officer who
investigated the accident in which Nathan had wrapped the car around the
utility pole came by my home. I invited him in, and we sat in the living
room and talked for quite some time.

He felt genuinely bad that he had to give me the ticket for owning a
vehicle whose driver had left the scene of an accident. But because there
were no witnesses to verify Nathan had been the driver, as the registered
owner I was technically responsible.

He suggested I dispute the ticket, so I did write a letter, and a court date was set. It would be sixteen and a half months before the hearing would take place, and a lot happened before then.

That Nathan ran and that I had to deal with the fall-out is just sad and wrong on every level. But when it comes to drug addiction and those we love who battle addiction, we have to put one foot in front of the other and carry on because we have no other choice.

~ 33 ~

WELL CALL ME STUPID,
BUT MY HEART WAS IN THE RIGHT PLACE

"Perseverance is not a long race;
it is many short races one after another."

~ WALTER ELLIOT ~

WE HAD SPENT SEVERAL HOURS GETTING NATHAN INTO HIS various appointments, and I was anxious to get home. At this point, Nathan was going to be a father in just two and a half months. He said he was really looking forward to being a dad, and I just hoped drugs were finally in his past—that his new baby would be his future and he would make his son or daughter proud.

Earlier in this book, I said: "Wishing for something won't make it happen. When we are talking about addiction, all the wishing in the world won't make a bit of difference. It won't change our loved one's behavior. Change takes work." I emphasized that we have absolutely no control, no power when it comes to our addicted loved one, but we do have control over how we will play out our role in this deadly disease of addiction.

Well, I forgot my own advice, and wishing stepped up ahead of common sense. What did I do? I bought him a good used truck and tools so he "could work and support his baby." I convinced myself this was for the baby's sake and that Nathan would step up and take responsibility.

Some people never learn. Apparently I was one of them!!

I wanted so badly for Nathan to lead a clean, productive, proud life. I wanted him to be a fair and responsible co-parent with Ali, and above all, I wanted him to be the parent his child could always count on, the dad who would always be there—the dad I knew he wanted to be. I again put on blinders to the addiction.

~

As I mentioned, when Nathan got off the ferry his eyes had lost their warmth and there was an edge about him. Well, he was no sooner out than he began drinking and using. Within three weeks of his release, the truck was impounded for thirty days.

He was high and I knew it. He said it was the flu. Yet again.

I said, "Then you shouldn't have a problem if I call your parole officer and ask him to pull you in for drug testing."

He was angry, really angry. I walked out of his room, went downstairs, picked up the phone, and dialed his parole officer. Nathan was yelling at me to put down the phone but I wouldn't. His parole officer agreed to the drug test and Nathan was called in. He was furious with me.

It was 9:00 p.m. and I was exhausted, so I went up to bed. Michael was out with friends and wasn't aware of any of this. I didn't hear Nathan come in, or Michael and his friend later, but I jolted upright to yelling and banging coming from downstairs.

When Michael came home, Nathan was criticizing me for calling the parole officer. Michael is very protective of me, and he has watched this tragedy unfold for nineteen, going on twenty, years. He'd had enough.

"Don't you ever talk shit about Mom again. She has tried for twenty fucking years to save your sorry ass and you continue to screw her around." The fists were flying, the furniture was tipping over. I was terrified they were really going to hurt each other, and I told Nathan he had to leave. He started up the stairs and Michael went after him again. Michael does not like to fight. He doesn't back down from a situation, but he doesn't go looking for one either. He was just at a place where he couldn't stand for one more minute to watch one person taking down everyone.

He stood up and with tears in his eyes said, "Nathan, you're my brother and I love you, man, but I am tired of the bullshit. I'm not okay with you right now. Tomorrow I might be, but tonight I am not. Don't say another word about Mom. She didn't cause this today, you did. Just go upstairs and go to bed. We are not okay tonight." He gave Nathan a hug and then he went outside and sat in the dark. It was now the wee hours of Saturday morning.

Monday morning, the parole officer called. The tests on Friday night had been positive for cocaine and there was a warrant out for Nathan's arrest—breach of a parole condition. Again, he went back to prison.

~

While he was gone, I noticed several of our power tools were missing. I had to once again accept that without question, nothing we tried to do helped Nathan. You can't help someone who absolutely won't help himself, but when it's your son, you feel completely broken and powerless.

When Nathan was released this time, I had all his possessions packed in boxes. He could not come home and stay anymore. Twenty years of this and nothing had changed, nothing had improved, nothing had been learned, at least nothing I could see. In fact, the situation just kept getting worse.

Nathan sold the truck and went on a two-week cocaine binge. When I saw him, I was devastated. He had lost probably forty pounds, and his handsome face was covered with cuts and scabs and sores, as was his torso. Nothing he said made any sense, it was all disjointed babble. He was talking about clearing the snow off my car windshield, but there was no snow outside—it was springtime—and he was talking to "people," but there was no one else around. He was staying at a pay-by-the-month hotel, a place well known for its shady reputation. We had a cup of tea, I picked him up a few groceries, and I hugged him goodbye. Once again, I cried all the way home.

~

About a week later, Ali dropped by and spent most of the day with me. She wasn't due for another week, but she was getting more and more uncomfortable and ready.

Late in the afternoon, my daughter Kiara stopped in on her way home from work, and Ali asked her for a ride back to her apartment. Two hours later I received a call. Ali was hyperventilating and crying: her membranes had ruptured, and she was truly frightened. She said she had called Nathan, and he was going to run to the hospital and meet her there. He told her to call me to pick her up and take her to the hospital.

I told her to sit down and take a few slow breaths, and I'd be right there. I told her she was going to be just fine, that what she was experiencing was normal. When I arrived, I helped her get into dry slacks, then bundled her up, and we went to the hospital. When we arrived, Nathan met her at the door and up they went to the maternity ward while I parked the car.

Her cousin, a couple she knew, Nathan, and I waited with her throughout the night. At 7:04 a.m., Justin was born, but we were all immediately rushed away from the room and directed by security to a waiting area. A Code Pink was called and a team of medical personnel immediately descended on the delivery room; after a couple of minutes, they were able to open Justin's airway.

He was seven pounds, four ounces, and an absolutely beautiful baby, perfect in every way, from his lovely face to his precious little body. Aside from the initial scare right after birth, all had gone well with his delivery.

Nathan stayed with Ali and Justin around the clock for the few days they were in hospital. Nathan clearly fell head over heels in love with this little man immediately. I had never seen him more in awe, more in love, more at peace than at that time. He talked about the future, how he was going to be a wonderful hands-on dad—the dad who coached baseball and soccer, who threw the ball with his son outside after supper. He was going to be there every step of the way and would never let his son down.

And Nathan clearly meant what he was saying, with every fiber of his being. He wanted to be the dad who would be there whenever Justin wanted him to be, the dad his son could count on 100% of the time and be proud of. And he wanted to be there for Ali. He wanted to be a family, I don't doubt that for a single second. That is who he *wanted* to be.

~

Because of Nathan's history of addiction, Child Services would be monitoring Justin for a few months. When Ali and Justin were ready to be released from hospital, Ali asked whether they could come and stay with me for awhile. She was understandably nervous about going back to her place alone with a newborn. Since I had a home-based business, I could be available to her and Justin around the clock. She would express her milk and I could spell her off, feeding Justin through the night and during the day so she could get some rest. She was a girl who really needed her rest, and she wasn't ready to have Nathan helping out yet. We did the baths and fingernail trimming together the first few times until she was comfortable doing them on her own. It worked out well and she was comfortable.

When Justin was two and a half weeks old, Ali took him to visit her grandma for a few days, and when she came back, I encouraged her to move back to her place, but with the understanding that I would never be more than a phone call away. I felt that was important.

Over the first few months of Justin's life, Nathan and Ali had a number of issues to work on, all based around trust. They had both hurt each other in different but equally painful ways. It would take time, effort, sobriety, commitment, and understanding to build trust again. Gradually, she had Nathan help more and more. For a while, they seemed to be doing well.

Nathan was thrilled to be around Ali and Justin, and Ali was happy to have the help. They seemed to be connecting in a positive way.

Sadly, it was not to last, and Nathan had a relapse. Unfortunately, addiction is a formidable opponent. Nathan was losing, Ali was losing, our family was losing. But most important, most devastating, Justin was losing.

Ali and Justin moved away and initially did not leave any forwarding information. Nathan's relapse had a profound effect on Ali. She took being a mom as she should, completely to heart, knowing it was her responsibility to keep Justin out of harm's way. She decided to keep Nathan away from Justin for the time being. Ali and Justin had moved in with Ali's grandmother over on the island. She hoped to go to school. Her grandmother was going to lend financial support for her to be able to do that but it didn't work out and after a time, she moved back to our area.

Being a single mom is a huge responsibility. The blessing for Ali was that Justin was really a perfect little man, a very happy and contented baby, and she is to be highly commended for all she did to ensure his safety, well-being and happiness. It was not an easy road.

34

WILL THE VIOLENCE NEVER END?

*"Understand that your success in life won't be determined just by
what's given to you or what happens to you, but by what you do
with all of that—by how hard you try; how far you push yourself;
how high you are willing to reach. Because true excellence
comes only through perseverance. . . .
The truth is, no matter how hard you work, you won't necessarily
ace every class or succeed in every job. There will be times
when you screw up, when you hurt the people you love,
when you stray from your most deeply held values.
And when that happens, it's the easiest thing in the world
to start looking around for someone to blame."*

~ PRESIDENT BARACK OBAMA ~

WITH NATHAN'S RELAPSE, I DISTANCED MYSELF FROM HIM ONCE
again. He knew that I would do everything possible to help him get
and stay well, but that I would not help him out when he was using.

Eventually, Nathan found work at a factory. The job paid $12.75 an hour,
so it was better than minimum wage, and it was full-time. He was grateful
to be working. He had been employed by this company about a month and

a half when I went into hospital for back surgery. I got home to a number of messages on the answering machine, one of them from Nathan, left two days earlier.

He sounded dire. "Mom, I need help, Mom. I've been hurt with a baseball bat. I'm bleeding heavy from my head. Mom, I need help. I can't get up." Then the phone went dead.

I immediately called his cell phone. He sounded terrible when he answered. He was at his hotel room and said he could barely move; he was hurt badly. I called my friend Diane. Gina, her daughter, answered the phone. I asked them whether they could meet me at Nathan's hotel. I knew I would need help getting Nathan down the stairs and into my car.

When I opened the door to his room, he was lying on the bed. He was bruised literally from head to toe. He had staples in his scalp, and his back, legs, and arms were black and blue with bruising. He had been hit with a baseball bat eighteen times. His body was swollen from the battering.

Fortunately, Gina had brought her boyfriend with her, and we were able to get another tenant from the hotel as well. They were two big guys, and together they were able to carry Nathan down the hallway and the two flights of stairs from his room to my car.

My heart broke for my beautiful son. How much more abuse could one person withstand? When would this end?

Our friends followed us back home. Because Nathan could not weight bear at all, I needed to call on our next-door neighbor to help us lift him into the house and onto the couch.

What kind of people do this? What happened to them, that they lost their humanity? Initially, I suspected it was a retaliation for an unpaid drug debt, but Nathan insisted it wasn't. He didn't know who they were, he said. He had just come out of the mall, where he had cashed his paycheck, and was about to cross the street to get on the bus home when the attack occurred. It was a brutal robbery, definitely overkill, which was why I initially thought it was a personal rather than random attack.

If you or I were beaten with a baseball bat coming out of a bank, it would be front-page news. Every local channel would be carrying it. But society applies different standards to drug addicts, along the lines of, "They had it coming, they deserved it—and after all, they're used to it, and they're less than us, right?"

They are not!! They bleed just like we do, and they hurt and cry just like we do. Yet they don't get the same consideration because society has become so hardened that somehow it feels these are the addict's dues. But no one deserves to be brutalized, no one.

Nathan had to be off work for two weeks because of his injuries. Even when he returned to work, he was still in considerable discomfort, but was worried about losing his job if he took any more time.

Two and a half months later, though, Nathan left his factory job and told me he was working for a car transport company, positioning cars throughout southwestern British Columbia. He worked nights and said he made $250 a shift, paid in cash each night.

Red flag—I knew immediately this was something illegal and I told him so. No one, I said, makes $250 working an eight-hour shift driving cars. Most legitimate drivers make $10–14 dollars an hour, depending on their experience. And no reputable company pays in cash under the table after each shift. Legitimate businesses pay by check at regular pay periods and take off the legally required deductions.

I asked Nathan how he'd gotten a job driving for a company when he had DUI convictions; surely they must have asked for his driving profile. He told me they weren't concerned. Another red flag went up.

I told him I suspected he was moving stolen cars. He was adamant that it was no such thing, saying it was a good company, and even going so far as to say, "When we deliver the cars we detail them as well."

It doesn't take a rocket scientist to figure out a lie like that. I told him straight up that regardless of what he was telling me, I knew he was doing something illegal; I believed he was moving stolen cars and I strongly advised him to walk away from it right now. He was immovable: it was a good job and he was sticking with it.

I left him with this: "Nathan, you and I know that whatever you're doing, it's illegal. Eventually it's all going to come tumbling down and you're going to be in more trouble than you are now. You like the money the job pays, but this won't last. It's wrong and you'll be back in jail in no time. I am asking you one more time before I go, quit this job and do something legal; get a job you can count on."

A week later, he called to tell me he had bought a forty-inch color TV and wanted me to come to his hotel room to see it. I was disgusted, first because he was proud of buying something, despite knowing full well it was bought with money made from the proceeds of crime. He knows I have no use for that. Even more disappointing was the fact that when you're a parent who hasn't been paying child support, and suddenly you have extra money, you should be making darn sure the mother of your child gets that money. If he didn't want to give her the cash, then he should have taken her a case of diapers and wipes, a case of infant formula and baby food, a bus pass and a big bag of groceries.

A couple of days later, he called and asked whether we could meet for supper. I wanted to talk to him about this again and so I agreed. During supper he broke the news: it was a "dial-a-dope" operation—but he was still insisting he hadn't known.

As with Emelia's grandmother's necklace, which he had pawned and then "searched" for frantically, Nathan single-mindedly protested his ignorance. Deny, deny, deny in an effort to convince me he had had no idea he was doing anything wrong. "I thought I was delivering cars. I had no idea there were drugs hidden in the cars."

The denial was so off the wall and completely unbelievable, and yet he insisted and couldn't believe that I didn't believe him. Nathan isn't alone in this behavior. It is not an uncommon practice for an addict to become so obsessed with "proving" he is being unjustly accused of wrong-doing that he often goes to ridiculous lengths to convince you of his "innocence." I have seen it over and over again through the years, from addicted friends and acquaintances of Nathan.

Apparently, the night before, which was his night off, the dial-a-dope ring got busted and the other guys who were working that night were arrested. He felt lucky that he had "dodged that bullet," still insisting he had no idea. I was able to blow that lie out of the water when a man I had worked for made a "confession" to me. He was scared to tell me about it, because he knew how I felt about drugs and he was well aware of Nathan's addiction. But he is a good man, and a wonderful husband, father, and friend, who one night was willing to do something stupid. He and some of his buddies ordered cocaine during a guys' night, only to have Nathan show up at the door with the delivery. When the two saw each other, they were stunned, horrified, and embarrassed. He was afraid to let me know because we had long been good friends and had a special bond, but he knew it was the right thing to do. I respected his honesty and appreciated his consideration in telling me about it.

I knew. I knew.

Then came the next bit of bad news Nathan had to share. Not only was he out of work, with the dope-ring operation at least temporarily being shut down, but he had also been evicted from his hotel and needed to find another place to live—not an easy feat when you cannot provide references. Eventually, he was able to find another pay-by-the-month hotel, but he needed to sell his big-screen TV to put towards the rent.

Then the final bit of bad news: drugs were "missing" from some deliveries, and the gang he was working for was coming after Nathan to recoup the loss. He asked me for $1300 to pay these guys. I told him I couldn't help him.

These guys played hardball. He knew he was in over his head and was clearly afraid for his life, justifiably. He started hiding out. I hadn't heard from Nathan for a couple of days, so I called the hotel, but they said they hadn't seen him for two days either. I tried calling again the next day. Still no sign of Nathan. I asked the lady whether she would mind using her key to check out his room. I didn't know which was the greater worry: finding Nathan injured or dead from an overdose. The woman said she would check it out and call me back.

She called back within the hour. Nathan wasn't there, but they wanted his belongings packed up and gone. The room had syringes, spoons, other drug paraphernalia and was a mess. I apologized and said I'd be there after work to pack up the room and clean it up. She called again two hours later to tell me not to worry about coming to clean up, she'd already had the girl who cleans the hotel do it. I would just need to come and get Nathan's belongings. I felt badly they'd had to clean up that mess, so I brought Starbucks gift cards for her and for the girl. They appreciated the gesture. I appreciated them.

All his clothes were filthy. Several of his white socks had blood on them, so I knew he was injecting in his feet now; the veins in his arms had long ago collapsed. I needed to leave the duffle bag of clothes outside on the deck, the smell was so nauseating. I sorted it all out on the deck and brought in one washing machine load at a time. When the clothes were all washed, I put the duffle bag in the washing machine, but I needed to wash it twice, as the canvas held the odor.

Nathan's clothes were clean now, but where was Nathan?

His fear of the gang over the missing drugs had become his reality. They had grabbed Nathan off the street and held him against his will for eight days. During that time, he was severely brutalized. He was also forced to register and insure several vehicles that would be used for crime, using his name—a common practice to keep the heat off themselves. That was just a drop in the bucket of the things he was forced to do, none of which were good. He had been terrorized and seriously abused.

After the eight days, he was released. He called me, asking me to pick him up and begging me not to bring the police. I told him he now had a number of warrants out for his arrest. While being held, he had missed two court dates, and bench warrants had been issued for each. He had also missed his appointment with his probation officer, as well as his required drug maintenance appointments, so two breaches of probation were registered with the courts. He also wouldn't be able to pass a drug test.

I drove to meet him. He was in deep physical and emotional pain; clearly, he had been through over a week of hell. As soon as he saw me, he started crying. He was a broken man.

We came home, and he immediately went up to shower, shave, and use a disinfectant. I gave him a garbage bag for his clothes, which were in tatters, then tied up the bag—clothes, shoes, everything—and put it right in the trash. Once he had showered, shaved, and got into clean clothes, he came downstairs. I had made some lunch for him, and we sat and talked for a while. It was Sunday, and he agreed he would turn himself in at his probation office first thing Monday morning. He then lay down on the couch and slept a couple of hours.

When Nathan woke up, he called a friend who was currently in a recovery house. It was early December, there was going to be a festive dinner, and Nathan was invited. It was half an hour away and he needed a ride there but would have transportation back. He said he was hoping that after he dealt with the fall-out from the missed court dates and required appointments, perhaps he could get into the same recovery house. I drove him to meet up with his friend.

Two hours later, his buddy called, wondering where Nathan was. I didn't understand. I had dropped him off, but he hadn't shown up. I never heard anything from him all night. I was worried the guys that had held him had grabbed him off the street again. Once I hadn't heard anything by mid-morning the following day, I called the RCMP and reported Nathan as missing. When an officer arrived at my home, I told him all that I knew from what had transpired over the last few weeks.

Later that day, I had a call from Nathan telling me "not to worry." I called the officer back and told him I had heard from Nathan but had no idea where he was. He appeared to be "missing" by his own choice.

I didn't hear from Nathan again for over a week. When he finally called, he wanted help. I told him I would only help him turn himself in. By now, he had missed another court date, and another breach had been registered on his file. Legally, things were getting worse every day he failed to turn himself in. Physically, he was getting sicker every day he failed to turn himself in. His feet were badly infected from all the injecting, and emotionally he was drained.

He agreed to turn himself in on one condition and one condition only: if I gave him $80 for a shot of heroin so he wouldn't be detoxing during processing at the jail. He said he would start to detox once he was in a cell. He was clearly drug-sick and said he was in "a hunting mode," watching people to see whom he could rob to get the money needed for a fix. I wanted him off the street and back incarcerated. He would be safer and so would society. There was absolutely nothing I could do or say that would convince him to let me pick him up and take him to the jail. He was adamant that he would only allow me to do that if I paid for that fix.

Sometimes where drug addiction is concerned, we have to make a deal with the devil. This was one of those times: it was agree to buy the heroin and get him off the street, or say no and have no control at all over what could potentially unfold. I absolutely did not want anyone else to become collateral damage, to become a victim of his drug addiction.

So, I agreed.

I would pick him up at a designated spot, take him to his dealer, and pay $80 for his fix. If he did not live up to his part of the agreement—allowing me to take him to the RCMP detachment to turn himself in—I told him I would call the police and give them the location to find him. Obviously, it would be in his best interest to turn himself in.

We had a deal.

He asked me to bring Febreeze, an air freshener, so he could spray his clothes when I picked him up. He smelled terrible after being in the same clothes for a week and a half. His feet were badly infected and smelled like rotting meat.

He sprayed the Febreeze, clearly in pain and craving a fix in a bad way. I drove him to the dealer's, waited while he was in the crack house, drove him back to my place to shower and change, and then took him to the police station, and he turned himself in as he had promised.

The next morning, he was brought before a judge. He was in considerable pain from not having heroin for what was then eighteen hours. Eventually, he was sent back to his cell. A week later, he was released to a drug recovery house, but within three days he was returned to jail. Then he was before the judge again and once more released to a recovery house, only to be evicted two days later. He was again brought before the judge, who this time sent him to a provincial prison, where he stayed for six weeks.

While there, another inmate pulled a shank on him in the lunch lineup. He was able to get the shank away and, according to Nathan, a fight broke out between them before guards were able to break it up. As with any time there is a fight to that degree, the prison goes into lockdown. Nathan and the inmate who had the shank were both put "in the hole"—solitary confinement. Nathan was in there for five days. He said it was hell, never knowing whether it was night or day, or how much time was passing. He told me that if that wasn't enough for him to vow never to go back, he didn't know what was.

When he was released from that prison, he was on a waiting list to get into another treatment centre, but before that happened he went out and started using again.

As is all too often the case with those battling addiction, Nathan's comment to me was, "It wasn't my fault. A guy put something in my drink."

Possible? Of course.

Likely? No!

When trust has been broken time and time and time again, we have to err on the side of caution, and we are generally correct to do so.

35

THERE IS ONLY UP FROM WHERE THEY'VE BEEN, AND THERE IS ONLY UP FROM WHERE THEIR CHOICES HAVE TAKEN US

"I have come to realize that by 'helping,' we give them permission to use us, and we deny them the 'right' to take control and responsibility for their own decisions, own choices, own actions."

~ JUNE ARIANO-JAKES ~

*B*EFORE I WAS TO OFFER NATHAN ONE MORE OPPORTUNITY at a treatment program, I called Edgewood in Nanaimo and Narconon in Trois Rivière to see whether he could be readmitted to their programs, considering he had previously been asked to leave both organizations. I didn't want to mention it to Nathan until I knew whether there was a possibility. Both treatment centers got back to me within twelve hours and said they would definitely consider having Nathan back, but needed to speak with him at length first. They also said that if he agreed it was with the understanding that he had to make a commitment to remain in the program for a minimum of five months because of the degree of his addiction.

The next step was speaking with his probation officer, a really lovely, caring woman. I asked her whether, if Nathan agreed to go into either of these treatment facilities, she would be able to approve the move.

She said, "Absolutely. But June, because he is in the system, we have two approved treatment centers in the province that would be paid for if Nathan agreed to go to them. You wouldn't need to put more money into another treatment program and take that huge risk of losing what is left of your home."

That certainly sounded good to me, as my home was so heavily mortgaged that another loan against it would put me in a very precarious position.

I invited Nathan over to discuss all four possible options. Initially, he said he had made arrangements to get into another recovery house. Over the years, he has been in dozens of them—always being asked to leave because of behavior or attitude, just as he had been before his last incarceration. The likelihood of him remaining in any was slim to none. So I stressed the advantages of the treatment facilities, emphasizing that two I would be financially liable for and two Corrections would pay for. He immediately ruled out the latter two but agreed to talk to the other two.

He spoke to the intake coordinators at both facilities and made his decision. The cost to me would be about $40,000, covering the program, taxes, and money put into his account for incidentals, medication, physiotherapy, transportation to the facility, etc.

As soon as he told me his decision, he asked whether I would buy him new jeans. I explained I would have absolutely no extra money, and anyway he had a few pairs of jeans.

He said, "Okay, but I need new workout wear." I reminded him he had workout wear. His comment was, "But they're too baggy, I need new ones. You can get them at Walmart, they won't be too expensive there. I also need you to get my iPod out of the pawn shop, and Michael has to download fifty songs I have on a list I made up. I'll need some cartons of cigarettes to take with me, and money has to go into my account there in case we go out to a movie or something."

I tossed and turned all night. Not once in our discussion had Nathan even mentioned giving it his all or being grateful for another opportunity. Nor would he even consider that he had two options that wouldn't financially break me. It was all about "this is what you have to do and this is what I need and what you have to get me."

After lying there sleepless, I realized I was going to put the balance of my home up as collateral, but I had not heard one word about sobriety or another opportunity, and I saw that nothing had changed from every other time.

I do understand that the addict's thinking is selfish, but I needed something. Yet it seemed like Nathan saw this as perhaps more about getting away for awhile. Whether my sense was real or misunderstood, I had to acknowledge it, so I decided to talk to Nathan. I suggested it would be better if he went to one of the treatment centers Corrections was willing to sponsor, explaining my concerns I had had throughout the night.

Needless to say, Nathan was angry and adamant that he would not go to the other centers, even though they are well respected facilities. It was the one he chose or none. Again, it wasn't so much about him going to treatment as it was about going away, like so many times in the past. I always wanted his wellness much more than he did.

~

I have absolutely no doubt in my mind: Nathan wants to be clean, sober, and living a positive and healthy life. Of course he does. He doesn't want to be an addict, active in his addiction. Addiction is a very sad, painful, lonely, heart-breaking existence, and for whatever reason he just hasn't put in the work necessary to get out. It's that marathon, all uphill, that looks too daunting. And it *is* daunting. If it were easy, there would be no addicts.

Yet everything worth achieving takes work, commitment, the willingness to do whatever has to be done. Nothing compares when our very survival depends on it. That commitment is imperative.

I read an article once—it was actually about losing weight and getting fit. One sentence stuck in my mind: "Change happens when motivation outweighs complacency."

That one line can reflect on any aspect of our lives in which change is needed. *Perhaps more important, though, is in the life of an addict—and perhaps most important, in the lives of those of us who love them.*

Later that day, I drove Nathan to visit his son, Justin. Ali allowed Nathan to visit Justin in the afternoon. This was the first visit in several months and it was Justin's first birthday. Nathan was truly happy. I drove him to the coffee shop where they would meet.

Nathan had not been a presence in Justin's life because of the "selfishness" of addiction and then the profound feelings of shame from relapses. He has told me he doesn't feel "worthy" of a relationship with Justin until he has "something positive to bring to the table—something to offer."

If only the addict in our lives would realize each day gives the opportunity for a new beginning. They cannot rewrite the past, but they are the author of their future. It is time to begin working on becoming "worthy."

Yes, Nathan has a number of obstacles to navigate. Lack of education, a long history of addiction, anxiety, lack of credible references for a work history when he has never stayed with a job more than a couple of months because of addiction relapses. Lack of housing and character references. A history with the criminal justice system, including federal inmate status. Homelessness. All of these limit his job prospects. He needs someone to give him a chance to prove himself. But he needs to prove himself worthy first. This is a lot to overcome.

Nathan is working very hard at that—he has been clean and sober now for many months, but he still struggles with life, trying to get on his feet. Addiction has truly "beaten him up" and his sense of self-esteem is very low. The guilt and feelings of shame are overwhelming to him at times. But I know he is a good and kind man under all that baggage. I believe in him. His brother Michael believes in him. Now he just has to believe in himself.

I believe before we can move forward, we have to look at our past, acknowledge it for whatever it was, commit to healthy change and then forgive ourselves.

~

Ali is a genuinely kind, forgiving and understanding person, and I believe that when the day comes that Nathan is able to pick up the phone and call her, when he feels "worthy," Ali will give him the opportunity to be a part of Justin's life. In the meantime, Ali remembers her own painful childhood and is determined to insure Justin's childhood is safe, healthy and happy, and she is making it so.

~

I felt tremendous, overwhelming guilt that I had let him down. It didn't matter that it was the only logical decision I felt I could make. My chest felt heavy and it was hard to breathe. I don't let people down. I especially don't let Nathan down. I have never made a commitment to Nathan and changed my mind. I'd let myself down plenty of times, but not him.

I questioned whether I was making the right decision. I knew I was, but somehow it didn't feel completely right. Certainly my son was worth more to me than any amount of money. I would do anything to help him get well. But I had to question whether he was willing to do anything to help himself get well.

Addiction is a consummately selfish disease. To addicts, everything is about them. They really don't consider all the collateral damage, all the losses that those who love them have had to endure. That doesn't matter. The end always justifies the means. But nonetheless, my guilt felt all consuming.

~

A few hours later, when I picked Nathan up from his visit with Ali and Justin, we talked some more. He still was not willing to even consider the other centers.

He felt I had taken away the opportunity for him to get into the recovery house he was thinking about entering when I offered him the treatment center opportunity. According to him, I had left him high and dry. I told him that I would pay for two nights' accommodation, but only two, because he did have the option of going into treatment—just not the one he wanted to go to across the country.

The last two hotels he had been in would no longer rent to him. We went to a third. As soon as we walked in the door, the fellow behind the desk stood up and said he wouldn't rent to Nathan because he had caused too much trouble in the past. He didn't indicate what that trouble had been, and Nathan didn't volunteer that information. I was disgusted and very disappointed. These were family-run hotels, yet he had abused the right to stay in them.

There was one hotel left to try. I knew he had stayed there as well and caused issues, but maybe enough time had passed. Frustrated by this point, I said, "Nathan, if we can't get a room for you here then I will take you to a shelter."

"Thanks for nothing."

I knew he was angry that I wouldn't just let him stay back at home. But he had lost that privilege.

We were able to rent a room at the last hotel. I paid for the room and gave him a bag with bread, peanut butter, oranges, and salad. It was obvious that he thought very little of me right then. I pulled out of the parking lot and reminded myself again: "Change happens when motivation outweighs complacency."

~

A couple of days later, he went into the recovery house he was interested in. He stayed there about two weeks then left, for what reason I don't know. A few weeks later, he checked into a detox facility and made arrangements to go into a treatment center after detoxing.

In the past when he was willing to go into a recovery house or treatment centre, it was most often because he either found himself homeless or had drug dealers or the police after him.

This time, I told him I would not take his calls—he would have to be clean and sober for six months before I would. Each and every time Nathan had been in a detox facility, a recovery house, or a treatment center, I had encouraged him in all ways. I had followed recommendations from the facilities, I had encouraged him to stay the course and told him how proud I was of his efforts. I had visited at visiting times and taken part in the programs offered. This time, as difficult as it was, I had to walk a different path.

~

Some years back, I took a wonderful program called Insite, at Edgewood Treatment Center, in Nanaimo. I heard a story that, if I remember correctly, was originally told by author Melody Beattie. The story went something like this: A man is walking down the sidewalk. There is a hole in the sidewalk, and the man trips and falls. The next day, he goes for his walk again. Forgetting about the hole in the sidewalk, he once again trips and falls. The third day, he goes for his walk again, but this time he remembers there is a hole in the sidewalk, and as he approaches, he is careful to step around it. The fourth day, the man gets ready for his walk. This time, he takes a different route.

Well this time, *I* will take a different route. I wish I could be there, openly cheering him on in his recovery. I want nothing more for him than to have a happy, healthy life, clean and sober, with drugs being only a distant memory. But all the many, many times before, he always stayed just long enough to get clean and healthy again, put on some weight and get some new clothes, and then out he would go again and use.

So I must take a different route because the old route just has too many holes to fall into.

Nathan knows deep down that I am in his corner, rooting for him. If he doesn't admit to that right now, in time he will. We can only have a healthy adult relationship if he stays clean and sober—when he is ready and willing to do whatever it takes to become the man who truly is inside. That man is there, I know it. I am waiting to meet him.

~ 36 ~

RELAPSE AND RELAPSE PREVENTION

*"Life with limits is often a choice.
Don't put a limit on your possibilities."*

~ JUNE ARIANO-JAKES ~

ELAPSE UNFORTUNATELY IS ALL TOO OFTEN PART OF THE journey to recovery, and recovery is itself a life-long journey. The addict's path can be one of successes and relapses. I would never say successes and failures, because each time an addict relapses, he hopefully learns something from it. It's a learning curve.

Recovery is like running a marathon entirely uphill. All recovering addicts have stumbled at points in their recovery. The difference between an addict in recovery and one who hasn't yet grabbed that life-line is that the addict in recovery has gotten back up and dug and clawed the way up that forbidding hill, along that marathon journey, always trying to reach the summit.

It can be done. Absolutely. Many, many addicts have been years in recovery and have wonderful, healthy lives with wonderful, healthy relationships. Was it difficult for them to make that transition from being a using addict to a healthy addict in recovery? Of course it was. Nothing has ever been as difficult. But ultimately, *it is a choice*: a choice whether to continue on that destructive and deadly path or to get off it and have a life worth living.

Stress is the leading cause of relapse. When an addict feels like his or her back is up against the wall in a series of negative situations, that call of (false) relief is always present. Whether stress is real or imagined, someone who has self-medicated is used to reaching for that fix to calm that stress, to "take away" that feeling.

We all know that stress is part of life. Stress is not necessarily bad; often, it's necessary. The addict needs to learn tools to control the stress rather than being controlled by it.

Environment also plays a huge role in relapse. The addict needs to find a positive, healthy environment. If an addict comes out of a treatment or recovery program and goes right back to old friends, the using environment, the old habits, negative energy, people who will sabotage the process, before long all those old triggers to use come flooding back. Old acquaintances, even sights and smells, can easily trigger a relapse. As lonely as it may feel initially until an addict develops new positive friendships, the old environment is toxic. It is vitally important for the addict to "open up" his world. By this I mean going to NA or AA meetings, and getting to know like-minded people who understand the journey because they too have lived it. Going for coffee, helping each other—fostering camaraderie.

Starting a hobby, joining a team, going to the gym, or taking a course are all ways to meet new people and expand one's environment in positive ways. Walking or running, riding a bike, going for a hike—activities like these help reduce stress and get those "feel good" endorphins working in the brain and the rest of the body.

The possibilities can be endless if a person is willing to embrace new ideas and new challenges.

Is it easy to make all these changes? Not at all. Change is never easy. It takes awareness, a strong desire, a firm commitment, a willingness to step outside one's comfort zone. And it takes effort, a lot of effort.

Meeting new people can be scary; it can also be exciting. Trying new experiences, embracing new challenges, can be daunting; they can also be thrilling. It is a matter of deciding whether or not to think of the cup as half empty or half full. It is a choice that belongs to each of us, whether we are the addict or the one who loves an addict, and each of these choices can take a person as far as he or she is willing to go.

This is an important point to emphasize: as much as all of these tools can help prevent the addicts in our lives from relapsing, these same suggestions can keep us from falling back into our old patterns of rescuing as well. Our loved ones may have taken the drugs, but we have lived the drug problem. To prevent us from falling back into our old patterns, we can attend NarAnon and Al-Anon meetings and talk with others who share similar experiences. We can return to a hobby that we used to enjoy before addiction took our peace and happiness away. We can go out and walk the dog, or call up a friend and get together.

It's time for us to get back to living. Addiction has taken as much from us as it has taken from our addicted loved ones.

NATHAN TAUGHT ME MORE ABOUT MYSELF THAN I EVER COULD HAVE LEARNED ON MY OWN

"Things don't have to be good for you to be great. You will face many defeats in your life, but never let yourself be defeated."

~ MAYA ANGELOU ~

NATHAN HAS TAUGHT ME MORE ABOUT MYSELF THAN I EVER could have learned on my own. He taught me that I never give up on the people I love. They may choose, for whatever reason, to walk away from me. That may be their choice, but it isn't mine.

He has taught me that I would walk to hell to bring him back, that nothing and no one could stop me. That my love for my son is so deep, I would rather he hated me forever and never wanted to see me again than have him die sick, sad, and lonely.

I have learned that I am stronger and more determined to challenge those who poison our loved ones with narcotics. Drugs are ruining lives every single day, and our children, partners, families, and friends get caught in that net.

Some of us are the parents of addicts. We love our children. That will never change.

As I have said previously, sometimes in order to help someone, we have to hurt them. When it is our child who is the addict, let us hope that this is the most difficult and heartbreaking thing we will ever have to do. That it will never be worse than that. That we never have to bury our child or any loved ones because of narcotics. And to those of you who have had to, I am so very, very sorry for your loss and your heartbreaking journey.

~ 38 ~

IF I HAD ONLY KNOWN THEN
WHAT I KNOW NOW . . .
BUT I HAD TO EXPERIENCE IT FIRST

"It's important that people know what you stand for.
It's equally important that they know what you won't stand for."

~ MARY H. WALDRIP ~

WE ALL LOOK BACK ON SOME OF OUR DECISIONS AND WONDER whether we could have chosen differently, chosen better. I know I did the best I could with what I knew at that time. Today, I have the information and experience of what worked and what didn't, of what I should have done at different times throughout Nathan's journey and mine, and my hope is that by writing this book, I can share that perspective with you.

For far too long, society treated drug addiction as "a dirty little secret." I am so grateful today for TV shows like Dr. Phil, Anderson, and Intervention. Shows that educate viewers about addiction, and what works and what doesn't. They have taken addiction out of the closet and shown us there is no shame in having the disease of addiction—it is a disease—the shame only exists if we do nothing about it. Active addiction is a disease with a choice, and only our addicted loved ones have the power to stop the insanity.

I am not saying what you should do. Each one of us has to make the decisions based on what feels right. What may have been a right decision for me may not be the right one for you. Only you know what you are capable of doing and what you can live with.

I know, though, that it is extremely difficult to maintain perspective when we are right in the middle of the chaos that is addiction, especially when the addict is someone we love so deeply. It is much easier to perceive clearly when we are somewhat removed—to see both the forest and the trees, so to speak.

I have to say one thing: give yourself permission to treat yourself the way you treat those you love, to take the same advice you would give a best friend if you thought it was needed.

Doing this is essential because otherwise we lose ourselves somewhere along the way. I know that I ceased to be important. So many problems and issues consumed every waking moment that there was no time or energy left for me. I put myself last. That was a huge mistake. It didn't help Nathan, it didn't help my other four children, and it didn't help me. When we put ourselves last, everyone suffers. Two of my adult children, Kiara and Michael, have since told me that they used to worry so much about me.

You may have done many of the same things I did: "helped" with rent, or maybe groceries, or car payments and gasoline when Nathan didn't have enough. It seemed he never had enough. *But it was and is wrong for us to do that.* Why? Because we keep them where they don't have to feel the consequences of their actions, since we fix the problems for them. *We* feel the consequences of their actions because it is we who go without—without a second pair of shoes, without a new outfit, almost certainly without a holiday. That is what I mean by losing ourselves, and these are just the things *we* see. We don't necessarily notice the enormous emotional toll, the heartbreak, the constant worry every time the phone rings. But those who love us and care about us, like our other children, or life partners, or parents, or good friends—they see, and it worries them deeply.

You must take care of yourself. Give yourself permission to feel or not feel. Shut off the phone and make a cup of tea and just sit and relax for a little while. These are "no-brainers," but in the insanity of this disease, before we even realize it, addiction has taken us hostage, and looking after ourselves seems like a luxury instead of a necessity.

Believe in yourself, and know you are doing the very best you can in a situation that causes unimaginable pain, suffering, and loss. You don't realize how strong you are until you walk the journey with an addict you love.

~

I look back at all the pain, suffering, and trauma that Nathan has experienced and know that if I had done some things differently, "raised the bottom," perhaps I could have prevented a lot of his suffering. By "raising the bottom" I mean not giving him permission by being so understanding.

Growing up, Nathan was never rude or defiant, never aggressive or mean-spirited. He was kind, likeable, and generous throughout his teen years and twenties. Sometimes I think it might have been easier if he hadn't been so darned "nice." You can get angry at someone who is being rude and mean-spirited, but how can you get angry at someone who says, "I'm sorry, you're right"?

That said, I have to acknowledge that he learned how to manipulate me. Each person battling the disease of addiction knows the right buttons to push and becomes very good at recognizing when to push them. Why? It's not that they have become devious people. They just know how to get you to give them the result they want.

For example, if your child knows how much you worry about his health, he'll use that card. He's drug-sick and lying in bed all day, but you believe he is genuinely sick—after all, maybe the flu has been going around. As parents, our impulse is to jump through all the hoops to make sure our children have everything they need to be comfortable. The next time this happens, you think he should go for a good check-up. After all, he shouldn't be getting sick so often. And you pamper him some more.

Later, he wants to go out and meet up with a friend. You really don't get the warm fuzzies from the friend, but your son's been in all day and the fresh air will probably do him the world of good, so you agree to drop him off. Just before you pull away to head back home he says, "Mom, is there any chance you have a little bit of money I could have, just in case my appetite comes back and I feel like having something to eat?" And of course, you give him the money.

So he got permission to lie in bed all day, then got dropped off to be with a friend you don't especially like, and then you handed him some money. It was a good con job and it will happen over and over again because it works for as long as we let it work.

Maybe your son or daughter has an apartment with a friend. You noticed when you popped in that it wasn't very clean, so you tidied up a bit. There wasn't much food in the refrigerator either, so you decided to stock it up for them. You just paid for their groceries because they had used their money for drugs. At the time, the situation seems minor enough, but it sets a pattern. Down the road, they can't make the rent. Later, it's a car payment. Before long, you are carrying them financially and wonder how you got there.

Is your son's bass guitar gone? How about the stereo system in his room, or his leather jacket? There is only one reason these articles disappear: they are easily converted into cash.

Is your daughter not paying as close attention to her appearance as she did before? Not clothes shopping or buying new earrings every paycheck? Losing weight, sniffling, has a new boyfriend that she doesn't seem eager to bring in to meet the family?

Are there times when your son just has to drive to the corner store to meet "someone" who owes him $20? Or a guy comes to the door at supper time and gets quickly escorted outside, and you see a heated argument going on through the window?

Do not, I repeat, do not believe their explanations. Start digging, and if you learn that drugs are involved, nip the problem in the bud right away. Shake everything up. They will yell and scream, "How dare you not trust me? How dare you go through my personal things? I hate you." *But if you think your kids are using drugs, be ruthless in getting to the truth. Your child's life may depend on it.*

So they hate you right now. You're supposed to be the parent, not their buddy. They will only hate you until they realize you helped them dodge a bullet.

Remember, trust is earned.

When your adult child or another adult loved one is clearly addicted and suffering the consequences of the addiction, you must "raise the bottom." I can say with absolute certainty that my son suffered twenty years, that I suffered twenty years with him, because he could not find his bottom, and because I always rescued him first. I thought I was catching him at his bottom, but all I did was soften the fall.

No, I am not taking the blame for my son's addiction—he chose to take drugs and unfortunately became a hostage to them—but I am recognizing that I certainly played a major role. I have to live with that knowledge. I would never knowingly hurt my son, but I did just that by helping him so much.

If he had been twenty years old, homeless, without food or warm clothing, wearing shoes with holes absorbing the rain, freezing cold, sleeping in a dumpster between cardboard boxes to keep warm, and had no one to rescue him, maybe, just maybe that would have been his bottom. He perhaps would have climbed up and asked for help with his addiction.

"But I couldn't leave my son with no food or jacket or decent shoes. That would have been unnecessary hardship. That would have just been cruel. I mean, I donate to charities. I give food to the food bank and clothes to the Salvation Army. Certainly I will help my son. What are you thinking?" I now know that by helping him, I hurt him. I made his life just comfortable enough to be bearable—so he didn't hit his bottom, and that window of opportunity was lost.

Tough love becomes necessary because we are fighting a foe so cruel, callous, and cunning, so heartless, greedy, and unrelenting that we will never face another quite like it. To addicts, drugs soothe and calm, allowing everything to seem good for a while; that is what draws them in and keeps them coming back for more. It's a con game, of course. Drugs clearly deliver a false sense of "good" while in actuality destroying the users. After a while, they have to keep going back just to feel okay. This is what they and we are up against.

I wish that I had practiced tough love twenty years ago—made it so difficult that coming home and staying clean was easier. I wish that I had gone to the police when I found Nathan and his friends terrified and huddled in my bathroom because of money they had to pay a trafficker. I wish that I had followed him every single time he left the house, and reported to the police every address he went into and quickly exited. I wish I had grabbed a baseball bat and smashed out the headlights of anyone who came on my property looking for Nathan.

I wish . . . I wish . . . I wish . . . Oh, how I wish I had attacked Nathan's addiction differently.

It may have made no difference, but then again, it may have raised the bottom so he hit that sooner instead of falling so far.

I love you, my son. I love you more.

~ 39 ~

TIME TO LET THE GUILT GO.
YOU DIDN'T FAIL.
YOU AREN'T TO BLAME.

*"If you're busy hugging the past, you can't embrace the future.
Don't let the past kidnap your future."*

~ AUTHOR UNKNOWN ~

*"You're braver than you believe and stronger than you seem
and smarter than you think."*

~ CHRISTOPHER ROBIN TO WINNIE-THE-POOH ~

WE ALL NEED SOMEONE TO BELIEVE IN US. OUR ADDICTED loved one does and so do we. If it is only you in the struggle, then believe in yourself. "I can do it!" is a powerful sentiment.

You have taken a brutal beating from self-blame, guilt, your sense of failure. But *you didn't fail, you aren't to blame*. You did the best you could with what you knew. Now, all you experienced, all your new awareness, allows you to move forward in a positive way. Be kind to yourself. Give yourself permission to take care of you. You are overdue. *You can do it.* You can. Believe it. Live it. Trust it.

We are influenced by everything that comes our way in life, the good, the bad, and the ugly. Addiction has brought the bad and the ugly to our doorsteps, but only we can give it the power to determine who we will be.

We deserve the right to have happiness in our lives, to have positivity. We should be able to experience a sense of joy, in spite of the overwhelming heartache of our loved one's addiction. Each day, make that conscious choice. *Your* need. *Your* right. *Your* choice. Remind yourself that you did not cause the addiction and you cannot cure it. Use your power to control what you can.

Sometimes it seems nothing positive has happened. So dig deeper. It doesn't have to be big. Just something that for a moment caught your eye and took your thoughts of addiction away. A butterfly fluttering by. An elderly couple holding hands. The warmth of the sun on your face.

You are not alone. I am not alone. It sometimes feels like everything is dark, but beauty remains. We have to start looking, even if initially that means making a conscious effort, a commitment to finding something good, something fine, something positive. Just take the time to say, "Today I will allow something good to touch my life, something beautiful," and it will surface.

We have been so weighted down by pain and suffering, worry and heartache, fear and tears, that we have missed things that still are beautiful, that still are peaceful. But today we will make a conscious effort to find one thing—tomorrow two and the next day three. Our goal is to see that as much as we cannot change the horribly heartbreaking damage of addiction, we are more than that addiction. In spite of all the hurting and ugliness, the world still has so much beauty. We deserve to see it and just enjoy an "awww" moment.

Go for a walk after a rain. Breathe in deeply. It smells wonderful and it is cleansing. Light a candle and sit in the stillness of the night. Even if it is just something momentary, take it.

Do not give anyone permission to steal all your happiness.

～

With every experience in life, we learn something. It may get filed away somewhere in the "memory box" of our minds, but it is there, and sometimes down the road that experience that hurt so much comes back and saves us from repeating it. It may take several times to learn the lesson, but we do learn and that lets us know what we will and will not tolerate or what we are or are not willing to negotiate and to live with. Every experience, good, bad, or indifferent, is a part of who we are and where we will go.

My son Michael asked me once, "How do you keep going, Mom, when so much has sucked?" To that I can say, some of the hurts and worries would have been unfathomable to me years ago. But I am comfortable in my own skin. I like the person I am. I know I am kind and honest and that I never hurt anyone intentionally. I know that when I believe in something or someone, I never give up. I am not a quitter. If I have learned one thing in life, it is that no matter how much the pain has and does hurt, I am who I am *in spite of* the experience and *because of* the experience.

I also accept that there are many things in life I can't change. That lesson has taken me years to learn, but that is okay because I have learned other things from it as well. "It's the journey, not the destination"—that kind of idea.

Think of climbing a mountain. Would you learn anything if you and a friend rode in a helicopter to the top of a mountain, stopped so you could see the view, and then returned to your yard? Not much. It would be easy and you would have seen the view from the top of the mountain, returning safely with no bumps or bruises, but you would have learned nothing from the experience.

On the other hand, say you and a buddy climbed the mountain, getting all the bumps and bruises, all the fears and thrills. You both depended on and helped each other throughout the climb. Maybe at times your buddy had to "carry" you, and at times you had to "carry" your buddy. You reached the top, looked down, and said, "WOW." You might well have seen the exact same scenery as the person who rode in the helicopter, but *your* view came with the appreciation of what it took to get there.

I think of that in relation to the journey we are on with our addicted loved ones. Like them, we may have made decisions we would rather we had not made. Many times in life, we may wish we had taken a different path. We've hated all the hurt, but we've loved all the joy. And that is what our journey—yours, mine, and our addicted loved ones' in their own way—is really all about. This journey has been so painful, but we've learned a lot of lessons along the way and hopefully, one day, we will get to see the view from the top of the mountain—that day when our addicted loved one finds recovery. And until that time, we carry on because they are worth it and so are we.

Walk with pride and with confidence, and remember that unless you have *intentionally sabotaged* your loved one's efforts, you have nothing to apologize for. You did the best you could with what you knew at that time.

~

Moms are supposed to be kind and gentle and loving, as are other family members, partners, and friends. Oh, if only we lived in a perfect world. But that is not our reality, because we have loved ones addicted to drugs.

If we can hope to change one life, our child's or the life of someone else we love, the journey may be long and there will be many obstacles thrown in the way, but we are tough and we will fight and we will do whatever it takes to help our loved ones become whole again.

I am deeply blessed because as long as my son is alive, there is hope. I no longer have expectations each time Nathan detoxes or enters a facility, but I always have hope and the belief that he can get a grasp on his addiction when he chooses, because in the end, it is a disease with a choice and only Nathan can choose the path he will follow. Every day, I pray he finds his power to choose the path he was meant to travel, that he deserves to travel.

I cry for all those who have lost someone they love to addiction, have lost the battle to bring them home. Please know that you have many soul sisters and brothers who pray for you, just as you pray for them. You know the ultimate heartbreak, and your prayers help to continue the fight against addiction and the stigma attached to it.

On the following pages you will find information about some of the many drugs being abused by our addicted loved ones. I hope this information will help you identify the dangers and halt this deadly journey, this living nightmare, so that others may come out of the darkness and into the light.

Drug addicts are not disposable commodities. They are our children and they are deeply loved.

Let us hope that one day, we will all live in a world where drug addiction is just a bad memory, where it is relegated to the pages of history. That someone, somewhere, working in a laboratory will come up with the cause of addiction and the cure, so that those who suffer with the disease will one day be free, and so that no families in the future have to travel down that horrendous path.

Thank you so much for the privilege of sharing my journey with you. I wish you peace.

Much love to you all,
Junie

~ APPENDIX ~

COMMONLY ABUSED DRUGS—THEIR SIGNS, ADDICTIVENESS, AND CONSEQUENCES

There are many, many different drugs being abused today. Note I am saying *abused*, not *used*, as many of these substances have medical benefits in a controlled situation.

Whether it is heroin, cocaine, crack cocaine, marijuana, OxyContin, LSD, Percocet, codeine, morphine, Vicodin, clonazepam, Seroquel, Ritalin, ecstasy, amphetamines, barbiturates, whatever, one thing is certain: if these drugs are being used in a negligent or reckless manner, are being abused by addicts, they all have one thing in common—they alter the reward center of the brain that is responsible for good judgment and sound decision making.

They affect the way we process learning and whether or not we are motivated. They affect the "feel good" portion of the brain. Eventually, the brain becomes used to that "high" and in order to feel pleasure, the addict has to up his or her game, constantly using higher and stronger dosages to achieve the desired affect.

The following offers descriptions of these drugs and their short- and long-term effects when abused, to allow you to identify the signs that someone is abusing one or more of these substances. I hope you will find this information helpful.

COCAINE

Cocaine is a powerfully addictive stimulant that directly affects the brain. It comes from the leaves of the coca bush and is processed to form a fine, white power. This is the form in which it is either snorted or first dissolved in water and then injected. It is usually diluted with such substances as corn starch, talcum powder, or sugar, or mixed with other stimulant amphetamines.

Cocaine produces euphoria, and as cocaine abuse continues, tolerance develops, meaning that higher doses and more frequent use are required for the brain to register a similar level of pleasure.

Short-term effects are increased energy, mental alertness, decreased appetite, and heightened senses of sight, sound, and touch. A person may feel more calm and in control, but the effect doesn't last long. He or she may be much more talkative than normal. When the "high" wears off, the person may feel depressed or anxious.

Other short-term effects can include anxiety, paranoid thinking, dry mouth, increased blood pressure and heart rate, nausea and vomiting, paranoid psychosis, and hallucinations.

Long-term abuse can have many unwanted effects, such as irritability, mood disturbances, erratic, bizarre, or violent behavior, and paranoia. Other long-term effects can include medical complications such as chronic high blood pressure and irregular heartbeat.

There is a potentially dangerous interaction between cocaine and alcohol, and the mixture of cocaine and alcohol is the most common two-substance combination that results in drug-related death.

Those who snort cocaine often have runny noses and develop numerous sinus infections. In addition, the wall that separates the nostrils can become perforated and bleed often.

Injectors of cocaine frequently develop viruses, including hepatitis B, hepatitis C, and HIV, from the sharing of needles and spoons.

Regular cocaine users most often develop psychological dependence on the drug.

CRACK COCAINE

Removing hydrochloride from cocaine through a chemical process is called freebasing and makes the drug more potent.

Crack cocaine is a solid form of freebased cocaine. It is called crack because it cracks and snaps when it is heated to be smoked.

Crack is used by placing the substance in a glass pipe, heating it, and inhaling the vapors. The vapors are rapidly absorbed through the lungs and reach the brain within fifteen seconds.

Smoking crack cocaine can cause chest pain and breathing difficulties, referred to as crack lung. Other effects include convulsions, heart attack, stroke, and extreme depression.

ECSTASY

Ecstasy is a street drug that is only made in illegal labs. It is usually sold as a tablet, capsule, or powder. It is commonly distributed at late-night raves, night-clubs, and concerts.

Ecstasy may produce feelings of well-being, friendliness, empathy, and close-ness to others. The effects of ecstasy start after about twenty minutes and last from four to six hours.

Because ecstasy suppresses the need to eat, drink, and sleep, it can result in severe dehydration. It also elevates the body temperature. These effects, combined with physical activity such as dancing and a warm environment, can have very dangerous medical outcomes, such as kidney or heart failure, strokes, and seizures.

Some ecstasy users drink too much water to avoid dehydration, which can result in dangerously low sodium levels in the blood, leading in some instances to confusion and convulsions that can quickly progress to coma and death from swelling of the brain.

Ecstasy can be addictive, but physical dependence is rare.

GHB

Gamma-hydroxybutyrate (GHB) is abused for its euphoric, sedative, and ana-bolic (body building) effects. Like Rohypnol, GHB has been associated with sexual assault. It is odorless and tasteless, allowing it to be slipped into drinks undetected.

Users or victims of GHB feel relaxed, euphoric, sedated, and sleepy. It also causes loss of inhibitions. Effects are usually felt within ten to twenty minutes and may last up to four hours.

GHB is dangerous and unpredictable. Taking it with other central nervous system depressants such as alcohol is very hazardous, potentially leading to slowed breathing and ultimately death because the brain stops "telling" the lungs to breathe.

There is a very fine line between the amount of GHB that yields the desired or pleasurable effects and the amount that produces an overdose. GHB overdose can cause slowed breathing, coma, seizures, and potentially death.

GHB can lead to physical dependence and to addiction. Withdrawal symptoms include anxiety, confusion, paranoia, nausea, vomiting and diarrhea, tremors and muscle cramps, difficulty sleeping, sweating, and hallucinations.

HEROIN

Heroin is made from morphine, a naturally occurring substance derived from the seed pod of the Asian opium poppy plant. Heroin is the most rapidly acting of the opiates.

Pure heroin is a fine, white, bitter-tasting powder. Depending on what other substance it is cut with, it may be white or brownish, or a black, sticky, gummy substance referred to as black tar heroin.

Heroin can be snorted. It can also be smoked, which is referred to as chasing the dragon; the effects will be felt within ten to fifteen minutes. When heroin is injected either into a vein (referred to as mainlining) or into a muscle or under the skin (referred to as skin popping), it crosses the blood/brain barrier within seconds.

The effects of heroin typically last three to five hours. Initially, there is the "rush," which is a powerful surge of pleasurable sensations lasting up to a few minutes; this is usually accompanied by a warm sensation and a heavy feeling in the arms and legs, along with a sense of relaxation and happiness, and the absence of physical and emotional pain. After the initial rush, the addict will be drowsy and very relaxed, which is often referred to as being "on the nod." Breathing and heart rate can be slowed, sometimes to the point of death.

Heroin produces a profound degree of tolerance and physical dependence. The risk of overdose is high and unpredictable because users do not know the actual strength of the particular batch they are using. A person who overdoses may fall unconscious very quickly after injecting the drug. An antidote called naloxone can, if used quickly, reverse the effects of heroin.

Long-term effects of heroin use include infectious diseases such as HIV, hepatitis B, hepatitis C, and tuberculosis, transmitted via shared needles, as well as collapsed veins, bacterial infections, skin infections and abscesses, blood poisoning (septicemia), infections in the lining of the heart, and arthritis.

Once addicted to heroin, the addict's primary purpose in life becomes getting and using it. The drug literally changes the user's brain and takes over his or her life. A person addicted to heroin finds it very hard to stop using the drug. Those who no longer find the drug pleasurable may continue using to prevent withdrawal pain. Withdrawal from heroin generally begins about six hours after the last use, peaking over the next twenty-four to forty-eight hours and subsiding after a week to ten days. During withdrawal, addicts are extremely uncomfortable and have intense, continuous cravings for heroin. They experience flu-like symptoms such as runny nose, sneezing, sweating, muscle and bone pain, abdominal cramping with vomiting and diarrhea, involuntary jerking of the leg muscles, anxiety and restlessness, insomnia, rapid heart rate and high blood pressure, cold sweats and goose bumps (referred to as cold turkey), and severe depression.

LSD

LSD is one of the most potent mood-changing chemicals. It is odorless and colorless and has a slightly bitter taste. It is often added to absorbent paper and divided into small squares, each of which represents one dose.

The first effects generally begin between thirty and ninety minutes after taking it and may last as long as twelve hours. The drug produces delusions and visual hallucinations, as well as confusion and disorientation regarding time and space. Sensations can seem to "cross over" in that the user may feel he or she is "seeing sounds" or "hearing colors"; these experiences are referred to as a "trip." If the user has a scary or terrifying experience, it is referred to as a "bad trip"; fatal accidents can occur during such trips.

LSD is not considered an addictive drug since it does not produce compulsive drug-seeking behaviors like heroin or cocaine does, but like many addictive drugs, it does produce a tolerance with continued use, and when larger and larger dosages are taken to achieve previous highs, the user is in danger because LSD is very unpredictable in its effects.

Further dangers to LSD use can include a drug-induced psychosis distortion: the user's capacity to recognize reality, think rationally, and communicate with others becomes distorted. This psychotic-like state can persist long after the trip has ended and can produce dramatic mood swings, from mania to severe depression.

MARIJUANA

Marijuana is by far the world's most commonly used illicit drug. It is a grey or green mixture of dried flowers and leaves of the plant *cannabis sativa*.

Like myself, you may have family members, friends, acquaintances, or co-workers who smoke marijuana. They are not addicted and they do not use any other mind-altering substance. They may not consume alcohol. Instead of relaxing with a glass of wine in the evening, they may smoke marijuana. Here in British Columbia, Canada, unlike the other Canadian provinces and many of the states of the USA, there is a very relaxed approach to marijuana use. I accept that reality, but I don't condone it. It is still an illegal substance.

At the same time, I accept the argument that marijuana users versus those who consume alcohol have a much more mellow, laid back approach and rarely engage in volatile or aggressive behavior.

Although cannabis contains many different chemicals, its main mind-altering ingredient is tetrahydrocannabinol (THC). The amount of THC in the marijuana determines the drug's strength. THC levels are affected by several factors, including plant type, weather, soil, and the time of harvest. The more popular form of marijuana is made from just the buds and flowering tops of the female plants, in which the THC content is much higher.

Marijuana is usually smoked in loosely rolled papers known as "joints." Some users slice open and hollow out cigars, replacing the tobacco with marijuana to make what are known as "blunts."

Others will use a pipe or water pipe. Marijuana can also be brewed into tea or mixed in baked products such as brownies or cookies.

The effects of smoking marijuana are felt within a few minutes, peak in ten to thirty minutes, and may linger for two or three hours. Lower doses of marijuana produce a feeling of well-being and relaxation as well as heightened senses. Stronger doses intensify those reactions.

Outward signs of marijuana use are red or bloodshot eyes, an increased appetite, meaningless giggly conversations, and impaired short-term memory.

Marijuana users experience the same health concerns as tobacco smokers. They are more prone to chest colds, bronchitis, emphysema, and bronchial asthma, and are at increased risk of cancer.

Other dangers of marijuana use include increased heart rate, loss of motivation, impaired judgment, diminished short-term memory, increased risk of accidents, and damage to the respiratory and immune systems. Heavy users tend to make more errors regarding details and have difficulty sustaining attention to meet the demands of changes in their environment.

Throughout parts of the world, marijuana is used as a prescription medicine for those who find it helps them deal with pain or relieves the symptoms of such conditions as glaucoma, the loss of appetite that accompanies AIDS, and the nausea caused by cancer chemotherapy and chronic pain.

Although marijuana is considered a "soft drug," many people seem to become dependent on it as a coping mechanism when under stress in their daily lives. While it does not have the addictive qualities of drugs such as heroin and cocaine, it can be considered a "gateway drug" for those who later go on to highly addictive substances.

METHAMPHETAMINE

Methamphetamine is an illegal, synthetic (man-made) drug made in clandestine laboratories with relatively inexpensive over-the-counter ingredients found in most grocery and drug stores. It is a highly addictive and powerful stimulant that affects the central nervous system.

It is sold as a powder that dissolves in water or as larger crystals of high purity. It can be taken by mouth, smoked, snorted, or injected, the injectable form being referred to as "speed."

Crystal methamphetamine (crystal meth) is the smokable form of methamphetamine and is a larger, usually clear crystal of high purity that is smoked in a glass pipe like crack cocaine.

The fastest effects are felt within seconds of injection or smoking. Snorting produces effects within three to five minutes. When taken by mouth, it may take up to twenty minutes to begin working. The effects of methamphetamine may last for ten to twelve hours.

Methamphetamine can make a person feel euphoric, energetic, and alert, with an increase in mental capacity and physical strength. As the effects of methamphetamine begin to wear off, anxiety, irritability, aggression, paranoia, and hallucinations can develop. When this happens, the individual is at a high risk for violence.

Regular methamphetamine users have what is referred to as "meth mouth" (severe tooth decay), as well as skin lesions due to compulsive picking because they believe something is crawling under their skin. They feel anxious, lose their appetite, and can experience extreme weight loss. Often they develop repetitive body movements, paranoia, auditory hallucinations, and mood disturbances, and about 20% of users experience psychosis. Psychotic symptoms can sometimes last for months or years after use has ceased.

With continued use, tolerance for the drug develops, and the user requires higher doses more frequently. Although there are no physical manifestations of withdrawal, several mental symptoms occur, such as severe depression, mental and emotional discomfort, lengthy but disturbed sleep, extreme fatigue, a strong craving for the drug, paranoia, and aggression.

Intravenous meth abusers also risk acute lead poisoning, as a common method of production uses lead acetate as a reagent. Meth use can lead to death from the rupture of a blood vessel in the brain, heart failure, extremely elevated temperature, seizures, and coma.

This is a highly dangerous, destructive, and addictive substance.

OXYCONTIN

OxyContin, also know as oxy, O.C., and hillbilly heroin, is the brand name of a legal, time-release, opioid analgesic containing the active ingredient oxycodone, which is also found in Percocet and Percodan.

OxyContin is available by prescription only, to treat severe pain related to the back and neck as well as to help cancer patients manage pain and improve their ability to function. Under a prescribed dosage, it is an effective pain reliever.

Crushing OxyContin tablets disarms the medication's time-release action, and when the crushed substance is snorted, chewed, or mixed with water and injected, it provides a quick, intense "rush" to the brain, followed by a sedate, euphoric feeling. The effect lasts for up to five hours.

OxyContin is highly addictive and as tolerance develops, greater doses of the drug are required to achieve the high. Withdrawal symptoms are similar to those for heroin: muscle and bone pain, involuntary leg movements, restlessness and insomnia, diarrhea, vomiting, cramping, cold flashes with goose bumps ("cold turkey"), and extreme discomfort.

Because OxyContin, like heroin and other opioids, is a central nervous system depressant, the most serious risk associated with its abuse is respiratory depression, which causes death.

ROHYPNOL

Rohypnol is more commonly referred to as "roofies" or "the date rape drug." Although it is used as a pre-anesthetic medication and as a short-term treatment for insomnia or to treat depression resulting from use of cocaine or methamphetamine, it has been banned in some countries, including Canada and the USA. It is, however, smuggled in from other countries such as Mexico, where it is still legal.

Available in pill form, it is crushed and mixed into food or drinks, and people may unknowingly be given the drug. When combined with alcohol, it can incapacitate a person. Rohypnol acts as a sedative, muscle relaxant, and hypnotic, making resistance to crime (e.g., sexual assault) very difficult or impossible. Another side-effect is retroactive amnesia, whereby the person who was given the drug can't remember events that occurred while he or she was under its influence. Overdose of Rohypnol produces sedation, impaired speech and balance, and respiratory depression, and can cause coma and death.

Rohypnol abuse can lead to physical and psychological dependence. It is sometimes abused to enhance the effects of heroin and other opiates.

~ ABOUT THE AUTHOR ~

*J*une Ariano-Jakes is the mother of five adult children and the grand-mother of four. Born and raised in a small northwestern Ontario town, she and her family relocated to British Columbia, Canada in the summer of 1988. For the next twenty-three years she worked by day as a Licensed Childcare Provider. Throughout that period, she spent literally thousands of nights poring over material in the search for answers to help her son battle what would become a twenty-year heroin and cocaine addiction. This is her story.

~

June is available to participate in panel discussions on the effects of drug addiction within a family. She is also available for speaking engagements at churches, youth groups, parents' and women's groups, recovery houses, and recovery meetings. She would be honored and privileged to be invited to your group or organization.

Addiction impacts every life, everywhere, in one way or another. We may be the family member of a person battling addiction, or perhaps a friend, coworker, or neighbour. Every day, we may come in contact with someone battling addiction, but we may not even realize it. This is because the percentage of addicts who fit into the stereotypical mold of what we think an addict "looks" like is really very small. Perhaps you had your car or home broken into. Perhaps your bicycle was stolen, or your wallet or purse. Very likely that was a drug addict impacting your life. We are all affected.

～

To contact June, please send her an e-mail or visit her website:

june@addictionamothersstory.com

www.AddictionAMothersStory.com

CPSIA information can be obtained at www.ICGtesting.com
Printed in the USA
LVOW091101310112

266246LV00005B/1/P